C000136337

A Fortune
and a Family

The paddle-steamer Heather Bell *leaves for Swanage from Bournemouth's first (wooden) pier after the destruction of the T-end in a gale some weeks earlier in 1872.*

A Fortune

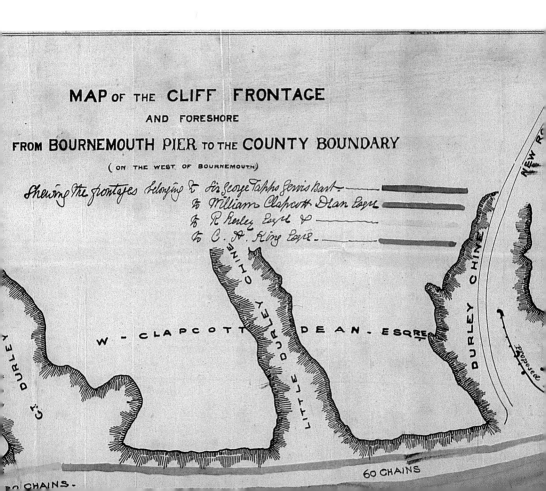

MAP OF THE **CLIFF FRONTAGE**

AND FORESHORE

FROM **BOURNEMOUTH** PIER TO THE **COUNTY BOUNDARY**

(ON THE WEST OF BOURNEMOUTH)

Shewing the frontages belonging to Sir George Tapps Gervis Bart ————
to William Clapcott Dean Esqre ————
to R Kerley Esqre &
to C. A. King Esqre ————

GT. DURLEY

W - CLAPCOTT DEAN - ESQRE

LITTLE DURLEY CHINE

DURLEY CHINE

NEW RD

Proposed

60 CHAINS

CHAINS.

and a Family

Bournemouth and the Cooper Deans

GEORGE BRUCE

Laverstock Books

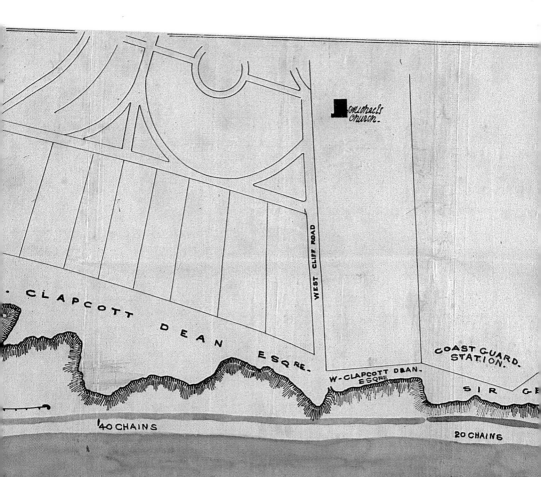

By The Same Author

WAR HISTORIES
Retreat From Kabul: The First Afghan War
The Stranglers
Six Battles for India
The Paladin Dictionary of Battles
The Burma Wars
Anthology: Short Stories of the First World War
The Warsaw Uprising (1944)
The Nazis
Sea Battles of the 20th Century
Second Front Now! The Road to D-Day

BIOGRAPHIES
A family Called Field
Eva Peron

BUSINESS HISTORIES
The Trentham Story
Polands At Lloyds
Kimberley Ale
A Wine Day's Work: The London House of Deinhard

Copyright © George Bruce, 1987
First Published in Great Britain
by Laverstock Books,
Laverstock,
Bridport, Dorsetshire DT6 5PE
1987

All rights reserved. No part of this publication may be reproduced, stored in a retrieval system, or transmitted, in any form or by any means, electronic, mechanical, photocopying, recording or otherwise, without the prior permission of the copyright holder.

British Library Cataloguing in Publication Data
Bruce, George,
    A fortune and a family : Bournemouth and the Cooper Deans.
    1. Cooper Dean (Family) 2. Bournemouth (Dorset) — History
    I. Title
    307.7'63   DA690.B685

    ISBN 0 9511896 0 3

Designed by Norman Reynolds

Typeset in 12 on 13½pt Plantin by Optichrome Limited,
Printed in Great Britain by Biddles Limited, Guildford, Surrey.

Contents

John Dean = Elizabeth Diamond
(married 7.10.1693)

Jane Reeks = Richard Dean
(1708-1756)

Henry
(1706-1708)

Lydia
(1702-1704)

James
(1694-1748)

John Dean = Mary Dean (married 1736)
(1715-1794)

Richard Dean = Mary Scott
(1742-1836)

Jane Dean
(1809-?)

Elizabeth Dean = Joseph Cooper (married 28.5.1832)
(1802-?)

William
(born 28.2.1835)

William Dean = Mary Dean (married 1767)
(1737-1812)

John Dean

Mary Dean

Mary Dean = William Clapcott
(1771-1854)

William Clapcott Dean
(1812-1887)
(no issue)

= Joseph
(born 28.6.1833)

James Edward Cooper
(1867-1946)

James Edward Cooper (Dean) = Anna West
(1840-1921)

Ellen Anne
(no issue)

Alice Elizabeth
(no issue)

Edith Bethia = Joseph Cooper Dean
(1866-1950)

Alice Ellen
(1899-1984)
(no issue)

Edith Bethia
(1902-1977)
(no issue)

Foreword

THE IDEA for a history of Bournemouth in the context of the part played by the ancient Dean family (later the Cooper Deans) of Holdenhurst, belongs entirely to Miss Sylvia Bowditch. She commissioned me to write this book to commemorate the family's vital but hitherto unrecorded and largely forgotten role, as well as their consistent generosity to the town and the inhabitants.

The story begins in about the year 1690, soon after the abdication of James II. The Deans were a family of yeoman farmers in Holdenhurst, the village often called 'the mother of Bournemouth'.

Mainly, it was William Dean (1737-1812) who sowed the seeds of the family fortune. In 1800, he founded, together with William Castleman and George Adams, the Christchurch, Wimborne & Ringwood Bank. He bought land in and around Holdenhurst; through the Enclosures of 1802-05 acquired a great deal more, so that eventually he owned major parts of what during the next 100 years were to become the most valuable areas of Bournemouth.

His grandson, William Clapcott Dean, was responsible for the residential and commercial development of these areas on the basis of plans drawn up by the town's first official architect, Christopher Creeke. Details of these plans are now published for the first time.

William Clapcott Dean having died childless, his cousin, James Edward Cooper, a master builder by trade, inherited this growing property empire in the burgeoning seaside resort and, a practical man, became closely associated with its favourable growth at the time.

7

Unpublished documents to which I have had access, covering some 150 years of the family's benevolent relationship with Bournemouth, have enabled me to give an extensive account of it and thus to cast shafts of new light upon its history.

For originating this history and for telling me a great deal of interest about Bournemouth and the Cooper Deans, I wish to thank Sylvia Bowditch. To my wife, author and historian Marie Louise Bruce, I am deeply grateful for skilfull editing, while to Mr Edward Stanley, who as legal executive had for more than 50 years helped to administer the family's estates, I owe heartfelt thanks. A mine of reliable information, 'Ted' Stanley provided me with some of the town's earliest plans, without which the book would be much less informative.

My thanks also to Mr Maurice Edwards for help with documents concerning the Alice Ellen Cooper Dean Foundation and to Mr Anthony Harding for kindly reading the typescript. Also to Ursula Wyndham for compiling the index, and to Bournemouth Corporation for historic records.

I am grateful to the staff of the Hampshire County Archives for access to Holdenhurst Parish records, to Mr Michael Edgington and the staff of the Lansdowne Reference Library for early guide books and photographs, to Mr J.M.L. Booker, archivist of Lloyds Bank, plc., for information and to the Bournemouth *Evening Echo* for access to the files.

George Bruce

CHAPTER 1

The Holdenhurst Years

FOR CENTURIES the Hampshire parish of Holdenhurst, called the mother of Bournemouth, nourished a branch of an ancient yeoman family named Dean. As yeoman farmers from the 16th to the 18th century they survived and won a measure of prosperity. In the 1800s, great wealth and local influence came their way, but in the second half of the twentieth century the family's last descendants, Ellen and Edith Cooper Dean, died childless. The family was extinct.

Families die out owing to the deaths of male scions through war, accident, disease, childless marriages or no marriages at all, although the end of one branch of a family is often balanced by the fruitfulness of another. Perhaps branches of the several families of Deans who once lived and laboured in Holdenhurst still exist somewhere, their descendants thriving. But the branch that interests us by its involvement in the creation and development of Bournemouth has gone forever.

For well over a century this family shared the Bournemouth limelight through their resources, their vision and their generosity. For the purposes of hospitals, schools, sports grounds, churches, public gardens and old people's homes, they made nearly 50 substantial gifts of land to the embryo town. Their decisions as to the placing and direction of streets, avenues and open spaces in their West Cliff, Dean Park, Northwood and Eastwood Estates contributed in so great a measure to Bournemouth that it would be true to say that their plans were inseparable from its progress and development.

If the parish of Holdenhurst is truly 'the mother of Bournemouth', the Deans were one of four families, with those of the Earls of Malmesbury, Sir George Ivison Tapps and Lewis

Tregonwell, Esquire, who fathered it. But in contrast to these families of the nobility and gentry, the Deans were simple yeomen in origin. How then, did they win wealth and power locally? What was their background?

Appropriately, this fortunate, yet ultimately ill-fated family, had both cradle and grave in the village of Holdenhurst. A fragment of the village still exists today, a vestige of old rural England, a scene of fields and cottages and a church seemingly disregarded by the march of time. Encompassed on all sides by motor roads bearing fast traffic through the suburbs of ever-growing Bournemouth, the visitor to what is today called the 'forgotten village' may imagine while standing on the green and hearing the noise of the rooks in the trees around the church, that he is back in the sixteenth century. For it is easy to visualise cottagers in smocks, carrying wooden buckets of water from the village well, drovers urging scraggy cattle out to the fields or hatted and caped parish worthies assembling in the shadow of the church to debate the maintenance of the Holdenhurst poor.

The Deans were not newcomers. They resided in Holdenhurst far back into the mists of time. The north choir aisle of Christchurch Priory holds a stone floor slab carved in Gothic capitals in Latin: *Tumba Johis Dene senioris de holnehurst et Juliane uxoris ejus, quorum aiabus propiciari dignet ds ame, qi Iohes obit... die... anno dni...* (Tomb of John Dene, senior of Holdenhurst and Juliane his wife, upon whose soul may God deign to have mercy, amen, which John died... day... in the year of our Lord...)

The mason failed to include the date of death, an omission that was never amended, but the spelling 'holnehurst', common usage in the sixteenth century, and the marked similarity in the style of lettering on the stone slab dated 1520 of Prior William Fryer's tomb, nearby in the north choir, is evidence of the family's presence in Holdenhurst when Henry VIII was meeting Francis I of France at the Field of the Cloth of Gold.

The abode of the Deans for so many hundreds of years, Holdenhurst village as it used to be and as it is today repays study. In bygone years part of the Liberty of Westover, belonging to the Manor of Christchurch, (Westover meant, originally, the west bank of the River Stour) it comprised six tithings, or rural divisions, four of which — Muscliff, Muck-leshell, Throop and Holdenhurst — were part of the parish of Holdenhurst. Iford and Tuckton, the other two, belonged to Christchurch parish.

Holdenhurst parish, which up to 1894 consisted of 7,390 acres, some 70 of which were usually inundated, gave a livelihood in the 17th century to about 350 families, mainly in the villages of Holdenhurst and Throop. Most of the men were agricultural labourers, but there were also a few smallholders, one or two shopkeepers, carpenters, thatchers and builders. In such a community, the few yeoman farmers were socially influential because the landowners, such as Sir George Ivison Tapps, who had inherited the Lordship of the Manor of Christchurch from Sir Peter Mews in 1708, did not often bother with parish-pump matters.

Holdenhurst was inevitably a close-knit community, isolated both by its situation in the extensive and desolate region which formed part of the Great Heath, stretching nearly to Dorchester, and by roads that were for the most part not much more than tracks. Its young men and women had little choice but each other for marriage in the ancient chapel there.

Holdenhurst chapel, mentioned in the Domesday Book, was built by the Saxons, and until it was foolishly demolished in 1834 to make room for a bigger place of worship, had been for centuries the very heart and centre of village life. Dominated as the men and women of the parish were by the ceaseless grind of primitive agriculture, it was the one single source of spiritual enlightenment, of something above their endless bodily labour. It represented hope, faith, love, the Christian virtues of compassion, charity and truth in an otherwise wholly unpredictable and sometimes brutal world. The Deans were christened, married and eventually buried there. Regularly, they assembled with fellow villagers to worship. In the landscape of their lives it was the most prominent and welcoming feature.

Tiny, even for a chapel of its time, it was built of brick and stone, a mere 25 feet eight inches wide, 33 feet long and 19 feet high, with a squat cupola topped on the roof by a short spire. A water colour by Benjamin Ferrey, one of the architects of Bournemouth and the historian of Christchurch Priory,

Holdenhurst chapel, seen in this 1831 drawing, probably by Benjamin Ferrey, was built by the Saxons and became for centuries the centre of local social and religious life until it was demolished in 1834 to make room for the more ambitious Victorian church.

shows it with a bell turret, called the 'tower' in the church-warden's accounts for 1688, kept that year by one John Dean.

The Deans in the seventeenth century, with the Dales, Reeks, Elliotts, Howkies, Edwards and Corbins were the chief yeoman families of Holdenhurst village, the first three being kinsmen through marriage. The Edwards family either came to an end through childless marriages or illness, or moved away from Holdenhurst in the early eighteenth century, for their name appears for the last time in the parish records in 1728. These records, which tell us much of Holdenhurst life, show that in 1688, John Dean as churchwarden, paid Joseph Troke, one of a labouring family that inhabited Holdenhurst for 200 years or more, eight shillings and seven pence for nails for mending the 'Speare', most probably the spire on the cupola. For lead, timber and boards and the time taken by 'Rich. Newland and John Gaiter to repair the "Tower"' he paid £12 9s 1d. and for two new bell ropes for the two bells in the tower he handed out four shillings.

The churchwardens and the overseers of the poor were appointed each year by rotation from the literate and prosperous yeomen of the village, like the Deans. It was their duty to control and keep the records of public spending on behalf of the parish, and to dispense the funds raised by a Poor Rate of one penny in the pound levied on all parish householders and property owners as often as it was needed.

Parish records show that from 1688, the year that James II abdicated and fled to France, to 1826, four years that is, before the death of George IV, the Deans held office either as churchwardens or overseers of the poor, 45 times, in which they were exceeded only by their kinsmen, the Dales, who did so 75 times from 1693 to 1813. The experience would have stood them in good stead in their own daily lives, as well as giving them an insight into the problems of their less fortunate neighbours, thus endowing them with the sense of civic responsibility and compassion they later brought to the growing community of Bournemouth.

Payments made by the Deans and the other overseers of the poor to the sick, the poor and to passing vagrants were generous enough in money of the day to trim the pride of our welfare state. There is evidence, at least in Holdenhurst, of a Christian spirit that goes well beyond basic necessity, or what was legally due, in some of the payments. When Mary Gardner, unmarried and probably old, fell sick in 1715 we find the entry: 'Mary Gardner, to buy her some meat against Christmas, two shillings. To John Boorn for Bleeding of Mary Gardner, 6 shillings. Wheat for Mary Gardner, £1 4s. 1716: For meat, soap, candles and Tobacco for M. Gardner, 1/6d. To John Holvey for looking after her, 8 shillings. Butter and cheese for her, 5/9d. Mending the lock of her Door, 6d. Malt for Mary Gardner, 8/7½d.'

By then, generously supplied with tobacco and with malt to brew her ale, Mary Gardner was doubtless well, but another woman, Margaret Gare was in need: '1713, Margaret Gare,

1 hat, 2 caps and 2 shifts for her, 6s 10d. Mending her shoes, 1/2d. 1716, A neckcloth for Margaret Gare, 1/2d. Mending Margaret Gare's clothes, 1/6d. 1719, Curing of Margaret Gare's leg, 11s 6d. A Handkerchief for her, 1/1d. Hosen and apron for her 4s 9d. A purge for her, 6d. Curing of her thumb, 5 shillings.' After which Margaret Gare was fit enough to move around, for in 1720 the overseers supplied 'A hat and pair of shoes for Margaret Gare, 7s 6d'. All seems to have been well for seven years after this kind treatment, but in 1727 comes, 'Funeral expenses of Margaret Gare, £1 2s 9d'.

The overseers, including John, William, Richard and Thomas Dean in turn, also paid the doctors' bills for those in need: '1718, Curing Ed. Pardy of an Inveterate Lepros Scabby Itch, £2 3s 0d. 1733, Curing Widow Chubb's dislocated arm, 5 shillings. 1749, Dr Hackman's Bill for curing Tarrant's Boy's broken Thigh, 3 Gns. 1762, To the Dr for setting Tremain's Maid's leg, £5 15s 0d. 1765, To looking after Will Best's burns and dressing it *(sic)*, 10 shillings. 1803, Pd Dr. for curing Marshall's Boy's knee, £2 2s'. Doctors' bills were high even in the 18th century, at least when the bill was paid by the overseers of the poor.

In Holdenhurst, worked also an unofficial 'home help' with the appealing name of Goody Critch, who from 1797 for 27 years to 1824, was paid much more modestly for attending the sick, sometimes at risk of her own life. When the children of the Dyet family went down with smallpox in 1820 she nursed them for several weeks, for which she was paid the meagre sum of £2. Not surprisingly, she herself fell ill but received only two payments of three shillings; then, on Christmas Eve, 2s 6d and two loads of turves for her fire, for the cutting and delivering of which Jasper Stickland received eight shillings.

In 1823, after a long absence, she again appears in the records as a Samaritan: 'To Goody Critch for taking in a woman ill on the Road, 5 shillings'. The last two payments to Goody Critch appear in 1824: 'To Goody Critch for her care of Avis Martin, one month, 4 shillings'. And finally, 'To Goody Critch for her care of Sims and Wife three months, 12 shillings'. How did Goody Critch survive? Perhaps she did not, for concerning her there are no more entries.

In the early 19th century, among the doctors who attended

the Holdenhurst poor at the expense of the parish was a Dr Goddard, doubtless a favourite among his patients for his thoughtful prescribing: '1816, Joseph Diet, six bottles of Porter @ 9d, 4/6. 1817, A bottle of Wine for Watton and Wife, 5/6d. 1822, A Bottle of Rum for Robert Troke, 5 shillings and a Bottle of Gin for him, 4s'. Best of all, in 1827: '2½ Bottles of Madeira Wine for Rich. White and his Wife by desire of Mr Goddard, 12s 6d'. Clearly, the doctor thought that the community should be kind to the less fortunate sick and needy.

The Holdenhurst yeomen, or, as they called themselves, 'substantial householders', who were appointed as overseers of the poor to administer this expenditure also provided clothing from time to time. In 1695 there is an entry for 'The Collins children; for mending their shoes and a new pair for 3s 10d. For a waistcoat and a fillit and three shifts for them 9s 1d. For a coat and a book for the girl, 2s 6d. In 1739, to Goody Seaman to buy her stockings, 1s 0d. 1741, an Apron for Alice King. 1785, for a smock Frock for Clark's Boy and pr of shoes, 8s 0d'. The criterion for all such payments was evidently need, as in 1795, 'one shilling for mending a sailor's wood leg', but sometimes the need was the parish's, as in 1803, '£2 Cash to Dobbing to take his family out of ye Parish'!

The overseers usually filled also the role of churchwardens, responsible for care of the fabric of the church, but they had other duties and strangest among them was payment for killing sparrows and other unwanted creatures, called 'vermin'. In 1689, Thomas Dean paid a lad 6d for three stoats' heads, for an otter's head 9d: for foxes' heads at 1s each, 14s 0d, for 'Polcats, Stotes and sparrows' heads, 3s 2d'. In 1703, John Dean and James Welshman, joint churchwardens, disbursed '2s for two otters' heads, 9s 5d for 57 Duzzen of Sparrow heads'.

John Dean's cousin Richard Dean, paid 11s 7d in 1702 for the bread and wine for church communion, although in 1709 when he was again warden the cost had gone up to 15s 0d. Money from the church funds was also given to vagrants, as for instance in 1715, '1s 0d to a travelling wench'. In 1700 the total paid out to 'travelling folk' was £3 0s ½d. In 1723 when, at 7s 0d, it was much less, the churchwardens noted on the accounts: 'We all protest against Allowance to Vagabonds for the

Future'. It seems they thought Holdenhurst money should be spent only on Holdenhurst folk.

During the 18th century, when nearly four fifths of the population of England still worked on the land, primitive agriculture was the main industry of the parish. The villagers of Holdenhurst, Throop, Moor Down, Muscliff and Strouden Green all worked on nearby farms, while most of these cottagers also cultivated their small plots, looked after their cow, chickens and pig, when not labouring for the tenant farmers and for the labouring poor it meant work six days a week for up to 16 hours a day every day of the year except Good Friday and Christmas. It was a crushing burden, and the weight of it turned men's minds to other, easier, more exciting ways of making a living.

In Holdenhurst parish, smuggling of contraband goods became, as elsewhere in the seaside southern counties, a great, unspoken industry that brought easy prosperity to working men, and to the nobility, the gentry and the yeomanry like the Deans, contraband wine, brandy, rum, tobacco, tea, coffee and fine cloth from France, at cheap duty-free prices. 'All classes contributed to its support,' declared in his *Diaries,* James Harris, first Earl of Malmesbury, one of the principal landowners of Holdenhurst parish, who was made Baron Malmesbury in 1788; Viscount Fitzharris and Earl of Malmesbury in 1800. 'The farmers lent their teams and labourers, and the gentry openly connived at the practise *(sic)* and dealt with the smugglers. The cargoes, chiefly of brandy, were concealed in the furze bushes that extended from Ringwood to Poole, and in the New Forest for thirty miles.'

And in *Memoirs of an ex-Minister* published in 1884, James Howard, Third Earl of Malmesbury (1807-89), noted: 'During the long war with France this wild country, which extended in an uncultivated state from Christchurch to Poole, was the resort of smugglers upon a large scale . . .

'The principal stronghold round which the smugglers operated was the sea-shore and its hollow cliffs that run from Christchurch Head to Poole, then a district of gorse and heath for 10 miles, with firwoods above them.'

In an anecdote worth quoting in full for the light it throws upon the complacent acceptance of the smugglers, even by the nobility, the third Earl of Malmesbury relates events in his childhood, at Heron Court (later renamed Hurn Court), an Elizabethan manor house near Christchurch, left to his grandfather by Mr Edward Cooper, a local squire, and chairman of the Customs & Excise. 'About 1780, Lord Shaftesbury was sitting at dinner in the low hall at Heron Court with his relation (Mr Hooper), the latter having his back to the window,' he tells us.

> The road passed by the front door of the house. Suddenly an immense clatter of waggons and horses disturbed their meal, and six or seven of these, heavily loaded with kegs, rushed past at full gallop. Lord Shaftesbury jumped up to look at the sight, but the old squire sat still, refusing to turn round, and eating his dinner complacently. Soon after, a detachment of cavalry arrived with their horses blown, and asking which way the smugglers had gone. Nobody would tell them, and no doubt they got safely through the New Forest. The smugglers had dashed through two deep fords in the Stour close by, which the soldiers had refused, and so lost their prey.

Usually well armed, the smugglers were capable of challenging and even beating off Custom's attacks. A local parson, the Reverend Richard Warner, recalled having as a schoolboy witnessed from time to time 'a procession of 20 or 30 waggons, loaded with kegs of spirits; an armed man sitting at the front and tail of each, and surrounded by a troop of two or three hundred horsemen, every one carrying on his enormous saddle from two to four tubs of spirits; winding deliberately, and with the most picturesque and imposing effect, along the skirts of Hengistbury Head, on their way towards the wild country to the north-west of Christchurch, the point of their separation.'

Richard Warner's observations led him to believe that the majority of families in Christchurch, Kinson and other villages were secretly getting rich by smuggling. 'It is scarcely credible,' he noted in his *Literary Recollections,* 'how many families were implicated, more or less, in this illicit and barbarising traffic; what large sums were accumulated by its practice; or with what openness and insolence it was carried on.'

These were the days before an effective counter-smuggling force was mounted, when the smugglers so far outnumbered the preventive forces in both numbers and arms that they could swagger ashore with their contraband in broad daylight. 'What could the opposition of a handful of revenue officers,' Warner questioned, 'have availed against bands of rawboned ruffians, hardened, determined, desperate and half-maddened with liquor, consisting of from one to three hundred in number'?

Warner believed that too often, only token resistance or none was opposed by the Customs men. Sometimes they made a secret deal with the smugglers which enabled them to land contraband in perfect safety even in broad daylight, for which they received 'as a douceur a trifling portion of those goods' which they were in duty bound to seize without fear or favour, laughing while doing so, over 'a flood of homely jokes' about the deal.

The inhabitants of Kinson — now, of course, part of Bournemouth, but in 1800 and earlier a tithing and hamlet of the parish of Canford — were almost to a man busy in the contraband trade. So devoted to it were they, and so highly did they rate it, that they used the parish church tower and even, the inside of a large altar tomb in the churchyard opposite the south door of the church for stowing away contraband, until that is, a churchwarden whose religious feelings were wounded gave away the secret.

Evidence of public sympathy for smugglers can be seen in the little churchyard there upon a headstone inscribed, ironically: 'To the memory of Robert Trotman, late of Rowd, in the county of Wilts, who was barbarously murdered on the shore near Poole, the 24th of March, 1765.' One would suppose poor Bob to be a Customs man, but no. He was a time-hardened smuggler, shot by the Customs in a skirmish on the coast near the mouth of the Bourne.

John Singer, a prosperous yeoman-smuggler of this same village of Kinson, made the spacious granary of his smallholding available as a contraband store to fellow *moonrakers*. The Customs men learned of it and on a carefully chosen day in 1780 when Singer had gone to market staged a lightning raid. They made a big haul, seizing no less than 541 gallons of rum or brandy and 1,871 pounds of coffee beans. But this was, of course, only a tiny fraction of the contraband smuggled successfully inland at the time from this area to cities as far off as Bath, Oxford and even London.

Singer is said to have been a secret agent in the smuggling empire of Isaac Gulliver, notorious king of the West Country smugglers, and outstanding in the history of smuggling. Described by Customs officers in 1788 as a man of 'great speculative genius', and as 'one of the greatest and most notorious smugglers in the West of England', Gulliver was exceptional for his character and intellect, no less than for his great strength and size.

Smugglers hid contraband wines and brandy brought in secretly from France in the altar tomb (foreground) seen here in Kinson parish churchyard. Damage to its heavy stone covering slab they caused when levering it up with a crowbar.

Opposing violence, he based his operations upon deception, forever hoodwinking the Customs about the time and place of his landings. Geoge Roberts, a 19th century historian of the West Country, tells how 'he kept forty or fifty men constantly employed, who wore a kind of livery, powdered hair, and smock frocks, from which they attained the name of 'White Wigs' . . . Till of late years, a chamber open towards the seat at the mouth of the River Lyme, was in existence, where the White Wigs took refreshment and remained in waiting until their services were required. This was about one hundred yards from the Customs House.'

In 1768, Gulliver had married a young beauty named Elizabeth Beale, believed to have been the daughter of the landlord of the Blacksmith's Arms in Thorney Down, on the road between Salisbury and Blandford. His reputed father-in-law, William Beale, evidently became one of his accomplices, for a Customs report of the time names him with Gulliver and one Roger Ridout as smugglers of 'great quantities of goods . . . between Poole and Christchurch . . .'

Having amassed a great fortune by the year 1800, Gulliver is said to have accepted a pardon on agreed terms for his past career, and to have become socially acceptable.

Such then, was the social and economic climate when the Dean family fortunes began to show signs of increase after unvarying centuries of similarity, during which even their names were limited, the men being usually John, William, Richard or Thomas, occasionally Henry or Robert, the women Mary, Elizabeth or Jane. To trace the descent of our particular line of the family becomes therefore so much harder. But with reasonable certainty we can follow it from early in the second half of the 17th century, and begin briefly with the Robert Dean who died in 1663, and in his will left 40 shillings to his grandson, John Dean, son of his son Henry Dean, and brother of his other son, James Dean. James Dean, in his will of 27 April 1663, 'gave unto his nephew John Dean the sum of 20 pounds. All his other goods and chattels he gives unto his brother Henry Deane . . .'

John Dean, richer then by the quite large sum of £22, married Elizabeth Diamond on 7 October 1693. John and Elizabeth had four children, according to parish records, the dates of which were occasionally guessed some time after the event, and then recorded as having taken place in either of two or more years.

Their children were James, born 1694, Mary, born 1695, Lydia, born 1702 (died 1704), Henry, born 1706 (died 1708), John, born 1715, died 1794. Fourteen years after the marriage of John Dean and Elizabeth Diamond, one Richard Dean, a first cousin, was married to Jane Reeks, in 1707. Curiously, there is no record of Richard's date of birth, but in family legal documents of the early 19th century the children of Richard and Jane are held to be first cousins of the children of John Dean (born 1706) and his cousin Mary Dean, whom he married in 1736.

The John Dean/Elizabeth Diamond and the Richard Dean/ Jane Reeks marriages were progenitors of the Deans, Clapcott Deans and Cooper-Deans who helped to set in motion events that brought about the creation of Bournemouth. From what might be called the lesser of the two marriages, that of Richard Dean and Jane Reeks, came a son named Richard, born 1709. His son, also named Richard, born in 1742, married Mary Scott in 1794 and they had four children, Elizabeth, Mary, Jane and John. Richard Dean's will, dated 1836, which happily has been preserved, throws some light on his material resources then. A yeoman farmer, he had evidently benefited from the agricultural improvements and high food prices during the Napoleonic Wars.

To his daughter Mary he left £100 in addition to the £100 he gave her on her marriage to John Dereham; £100 to Elizabeth in addition to the £100 he gave her on her marriage to Joseph Cooper, and to his daughter Jane Dean who was unmarried, £200, 'which said several legacies I direct shall be paid out of my Monies in the Funds ...

'I give and bequeath the Interest, Dividends and Annual proceeds of all the remainder of my Monies in the Public Stocks or Funds, of whatever description unto my Dear Wife Mary ... and after the decease of my said wife I give and bequeath ... my said Monies in the Stock or Funds of every description unto my said three Daughters ... to be equally divided between them, share and share alike ... I give and bequeath such part of my Household Goods and Furniture, Plate, Linen and China (not exceeding one third part) as my said Wife shall think proper to select ... absolutely for her own use and benefit in case she and my son John Dean shall not continue to reside together. And subject to the payment of my just Debts ... I give and bequeath all the rest ... of my property of every description ... unto my said son John Dean.'

John died only four years later, leaving property, mainly farm stock and personal assets, valued at £1,155, considerable money then. (A very approximate cash equivalent in 1987 may be obtained by multiplying by 80, but the scarcity of usable property of various kinds would increase the overall value greatly.)

It was not this branch of the Dean family that created the family fortune and influenced the development of Bournemouth. For the founding of the Dean fortune we must look again at the lives of the main branch of the family, headed by John Dean, who was born in 1715. For it was this John Dean's vision and energy that was decisive.

CHAPTER 2

Little Down

TRUE TO THE established pattern of intermarriage in the family, John Dean married his cousin, Mary Dean, in 1736, he being 21 and she 18, a date that will be more meaningful if it is recalled that George II had reigned then for nine years, and that the style of architecture now known as Georgian was in vogue.

Their wedding followed the merry style of the time. Huge white rosettes were pinned to the coats and dresses of the guests and tied to the coach-horses' ears. Coloured stuff, blue, yellow, pink, russet, was chosen for the bride's and bridesmaids' dresses, virginal white being a 19th century tradition. Fertility and prosperity being much in vogue, guests showered the bridal couple with handfuls of symbolic ripe corn, shouting 'Bread for life and pudding for ever!' By tradition the path from the church was strewn with flowers, rushes and herbs, especially rosemary, for remembrance.

Embarking on married life, John Dean was far from content with his status of yeoman, defined as one of that class of small freeholders who cultivated their own land; he dreamed of social advancement and the acquisition of wealth. It began to materialise when his wife Mary brought him a substantial dowry and his kinsman William Dean bequeathed him money and property.

It might also be guessed that he had perhaps financed smuggling operations, advancing money for the purchase of contraband wine and brandy in France, a transaction bound to show a handsome profit, because he soon had enough funds both to invest in property and to launch out in a small way as a private banker. He bought a cottage in Muckleshell from Sam

Hookey in 1749, when he was in his thirties, and a few years later one in Throop, from Henry Brenton. At the same time, he advanced money to local people wishing to mortgage or buy property — among them Peter Buffit, James Waterman, Henry Rooks, John Woolridge, Cornelius Trim and Samuel White.

He and Mary Dean were at this time residing at Carew's Farm, Throop, a farmhouse built in 1685 by Henry Carew, who had lived there until 1744, when Thomas Stokes had bought it and subsequently in 1761 sold it to John Dean. Ever more prosperous, John Dean then cast his eye on a neighbouring property. Little Down, as it was then called, comprised a house with several rooms, a few small cottages, gardens, barns, stables, outhouses and orchards, with 56 acres of arable land and pasture, all on high ground overlooking Holdenhurst and the more distant village of Christchurch. He bought it from John Reeks, a brewer, of Poole, in 1771 for £1,800, as an investment, then a year later sold it for £2,005 to John Strong, of Holdenhurst, a local squire described in the deeds of the sale as 'gentleman'; and Strong began to live there.

Although happy to sell the property at this very useful profit, John Dean was determined to hold on to something of the status that ownership of it gave, something that would perhaps help to bridge the social gulf between yeoman and gentleman, which may well have irked him. Allotted to Little Down under ecclesiastical law, was a large pew near the altar of the old Saxon church, beside those occupied by the gentry, and well removed from the humble cottagers who sat on wooden benches at the back of the church, or the lowliest of all, who had to stand.

As a churchwarden, John Dean doubtless had a seat somewhere in the cramped little church, but not a well-situated pew like that now occupied by John Strong, since his purchase of Little Down. Upon this pew, or at least part of it, John Dean cast covetous eyes. By argument supported by an offer of money he set about convincing John Strong that he himself, as former owner of Little Down, should be given a share in the pew. For one reason or the other, John Strong agreed, but his simple 'yes' was far short of what John Dean believed suitable for the transaction. He preferred to see it in the form of a deed

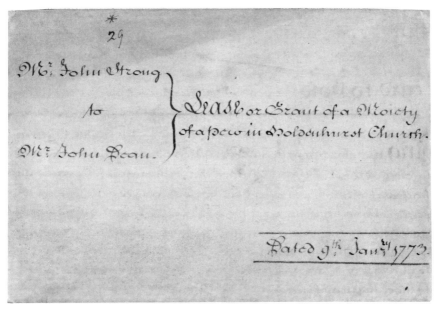

The agreement embodied in this document of 9 January 1773, covered the lease to John Dean of part of a pew in Holdenhurst chapel, held by John Strong.

giving him permanent right to occupy, as if he were buying a property, rather than merely being granted verbally the right to a place in the pew. So he had his attorney draw up a legal document for the arrangement. It is worth quoting in full for its unique interest as well as for the light it sheds on John Dean's obsessive attention to detail. It began, on a sheet of parchment measuring 18 by 24 inches:

> THIS INDENTURE made the ninth day in the Thirteenth Year of the Reign of our Sovereign Lord George the Third, by the Grace of God of Great Britain France and Ireland King, Defender of the faith and so forth and in the Year of our Lord, one Thousand and Seven Hundred and Seventy Three.
>
> Between John Strong of the parish of Holdenhurst in the County of Southampton Gentleman of the one part, and John Dean of the parish of Holdenhurst aforesaid Yeoman of the other part. WHEREAS the said John Strong is seized in fee simple of and in a Messuage or Tenement farm and Lands situate, lying and being at Little Down in the parish of Holdenhurst aforesaid, commonly called by the name of Little Down: To which said

farm and lands as incident and belonging thereto, there is a large pew or Seat in the parish Church of Holdenhurst aforesaid.

AND WHEREAS the said John Strong hath promised and agreed to grant and demise unto the said John Dean one undivided Moiety of half part of the said Pew or Seat, in such manner and subject as hereinafter mentioned. NOW THIS INDENTURE WITNESSETH that in pursuance and for performance of the said Agreement, and for and in Consideration of the Sum of Ten Shillings of lawful money of Great Britain, to the said John Strong in hand paid by the said John Dean . . . the Receipt whereof the said John Strong doth hereby acknowledge . . . HE the said John Strong HATH granted bargained sold and demised, and by these presents DOTH freely, clearly and absolutely grant bargain sell and demise unto the said John Dean his Executors Administrators and Assigns ONE full undivided Moiety or half part the whole into two equal parts divided, of ALL THAT the said pew or Seat in the parish church of Holdenhurst aforesaid, belonging to the said Messuage or Tenement Farm and Lands of him the said John Strong called Little Down, with free liberty of Ingress Egress and Regress unto and from the same, at all times of Divine Service, and at all other times whatsoever; and all the Right, Title and Interest of him the said John Strong of and in the said Moiety or half part of the said pew or Seat; TO HAVE AND TO HOLD the said Moiety . . . from the Feast of Saint Michael the Archangel last past before the date hereof, for by and during and unto the full end and Term of One Thousand Years . . . fully to be compleat and ended. YIELDING AND PAYING therefore yearly and every year during the said Term hereby granted unto the said John Strong his Heirs and Assigns the Rent of one pepper Corn on the Feast of Saint Michael the Archangel if the same shall be lawfully demanded.

This would seem conclusive, but for the painstaking John Dean it was not enough. Were his interests, he asked himself, fully protected? Might not John Strong seize upon some hitherto unmentioned factors relating to the pew and deny him right of 'ingress, egress or regress'? It appeared to him, or to his attorney, who was a kinsman, William Dean, that this was so, and that the Indenture was not yet fully watertight. The following was therefore added:

AND ALSO YIELDING paying doing and performing one moiety or half part of all Repairs and Costs Charges and

Expenses which shall from time to time be necessarily wanted laid out and expended in and about repairing and rebuilding of the said pew or Seat during the said Term hereby granted.

AND THE SAID John Strong for himself his Heirs Executors and Administrators doth covenant promise and agree to and with the said John Dean . . . that he the said John Dean . . . shall and may from time to time, and at all times during the said Term hereby granted, peaceably and quietly enter into, have hold use occupy possess and enjoy one undivided Moiety or half part of the said pew or Seat hereby demised, without any let suit trouble hindrance molestation interruption or denial of or by him the said John Strong his heirs executors and assigns or by any other person or persons whomsoever lawfully claiming or to claim by from or under him them or any of them, or by or through his their or any or either of their Acts, Means or procurement. IN WITNESS whereof the parties to these presents have hereunto set their hands and seals the day and year first above written.

Absurd as this legalistic fanfare about a seat in church may be, in fairness to John Dean it must be allowed that in the social climate of the day the issue was significant. Men of the same social class sat together, even in the sight of God. There among the gentry, for all to see, John Dean had raised his status in the tightly regulated society of the day, a gain well worth the expenditure of 10 shillings, the equivalent of about £50 today.

He was no less ambitious for his son William, born in 1737, who, given his background, might well have become a simple farmer. Instead, perhaps at his father's prompting, he decided to become a surgeon, which is how he was invariably described on subsequent legal documents. What formal training he had, whether he ever became a member of that corporation then referred to as 'the Master, Governors and Commonalty of the Art and Science of Surgery of London' we do not know; no records survive. And the Act of 1511 that prohibited anyone from practising as a surgeon unless duly admitted, evidently held sway only up to about seven miles from the city of London. William Dean may have trained in the wards of the then recently founded Winchester Hospital, or served some kind of indenture with a practising surgeon to learn the craft of setting fractures, or amputating gangrenous limbs without an anaesthetic more effective than two or three tots of rum!

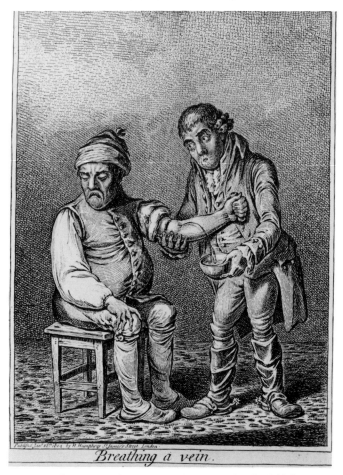

Breathing a vein.

William Dean (1737-1812) apparently grew tired of 18th century surgery, as in this drawing, published in London in 1804. Putting aside his bone-saws and scalpels, he turned to banking.

But we do know that as he grew older he could not have practised full time because, like his father, he was too much occupied with land and property deals, and with banking.

John Dean died, aged 79, in 1794, 19 years after his wife Mary. He was the first of the Deans to be buried in the family vault he had caused to be built in Holdenhurst churchyard, before the old Saxon church was demolished. Carved with garlands of flowers it is as fine as any there, a fitting monument to his ambition and achievement. He left nearly all his property to his son William, who was then living at Wimborne Minster.

William Dean's career as an up-and-coming banker coincided with the misfortunes of John Strong, who was finding Little Down an expensive home in the 1780s, in part perhaps owing to the land tax at four shillings in the pound imposed on houses above a certain value to help pay for the cost of war, notably that with the North American colonies, then fighting England for their independence.

John Strong now compounded his problems, and willy-nilly William Dean benefited. In May 1784 Strong had negotiated with William Brewer, yeoman, of Witchampstead, Dorset, a mortgage on Little Down of £400 for six months at four per cent per annum, the terms of which, should be default, empowered Brewer to 'peaceably and quietly enter into have hold use occupy possess and enjoy' the property, and furthermore to 'receive and take the rents issues and profits thereof to his own use . . .'

Thus, for a fraction of the price which he had paid for Little Down twelve years earlier, John Strong had now jeopardised his title to it. Having no ready money, he inevitably defaulted, and continued to do so. By February 1789, he owed William Brewer the then considerable sum of £475. In the words of the agreement reciting the events: ' . . . the said sum of £400 and interest was not paid to the said William Brewer on the day in the said proviso mentioned . . . whereby the Estate and interest of him the said William Brewer of and in the said mortgaged premises became absolute in law . . .'

In desperation, John Strong now turned to William Dean, the son of his old acquaintance from whom he had bought the property, and to whom he had sold a place in his pew at church. What then followed was entirely to William Dean's advantage. Strong requested him to advance the money to pay the £475 he himself owed on Little Down and to advance him another £300 on the security of the house. William Dean agreed; it was done, so he himself now had a lien in the property. It became even greater when Strong, desperately needing money, borrowed another £425 from William Dean, making a debt to him on the property of £900, which there was no chance of his ever being able to repay.

An unexpected turn in the sequence of events now followed. John Strong died suddenly early in 1790 and, since he had no

Littledown House, was built about 1798 to the order of William Dean of Holdenhurst, a surgeon turned banker, who, with George Adams and William Castleman established the Christchurch, Ringwood and Wimborne Bank in 1800. John Dean, William's father, had acquired the site some years earlier when it held a smaller house named Little Down.

children, his estate, including Little Down and the money owed upon it, passed to his cousins, Ann Kearly and her sister, Mary Hill, both of them married. Ann Kearly was evidently hard pressed for money, for a year later, on 25 March 1791, she arranged with William Dean a mortgage of £150 on the security of her interest in the property, making her debt a total of £600. But it was an impossible situation; to own Little Down she would need to raise a sum of money far beyond her power, so, in 1796, she decided to sell her half share in it to William Dean. The price agreed, very advantageously for her, was £1,700, out of which her debt of £600 to him would also be paid.

Only Mary Hill now stood between William Dean and entire ownership of Little Down, £450 of her half share in it being owed to him, but neither she nor her husband had so much money and they too decided to sell their share to him. A complicated sequence of financial transactions followed, through which, on 26 December 1798, the sole owner of Little Down became William Dean.

Having re-acquired the house and its surroundings, William Dean had ambitious plans for it. No precise records exist regarding the style or quality of the old house, but plainly whatever it was, he believed it could be replaced by something more in the spirit of the day, something with a fine classical façade. With all the zeal of a 20th century property developer, he demolished the old house and its surrounding wattle-and-daub cottages, having had designed to replace it the Littledown House that exists today. A somewhat austere medium-sized mansion in the classical 18th century style, three storeys high, it was constructed of stucco-covered stone with a wide portico of four Roman Doric columns surrounding a doorway with pilaster and window on each side. Apart from the flower-arranging room, the laundry-room, the kitchens, sculleries, the wine cellars, all in the basement, it contained sixteen lofty and spacious rooms, several of them facing south, giving a fine view of Christchurch Priory and the sea.

The new house, proof of William Dean's status of gentleman and squire, was conceived for gracious days and nights, for banquets, balls and leisured card-playing, with gentlemen and their ladies arriving in coaches-and-four announced by liveried footmen. In these impressive surroundings, William Dean, a one-time surgeon with both farming and property interests, who, like his father, had married his cousin, also named Mary Dean, now began a new career as a fully-fledged banker, having occupied his new home in 1800.

It was in the year 1800, when he was already 63 that, with two partners, William Castleman, an attorney, and George Adams, whose occupation is not recorded, he set up the banking firm of Dean, Castleman and Adams. As senior partner, he must have possessed ample resources, for it was reckoned then that a man needed a minimum of £20,000 capital to become a banker.

Unfortunately, the records of their enterprise, called the Christchurch, Wimborne & Ringwood Bank, no longer exist, so details of its transactions must be largely conjectural, but the bank prospered and we can safely assume that loans to notable smugglers contributed to its prosperity, and to that of William Dean, notably on account of certain family connections. William Rolls Fryer, a member of a well-known Dorset banking family at that time, who was associated with the bank, had married Elizabeth Gulliver, daughter of the notorious smuggler. And their daughter, Ann Fryer, married Edward Castleman, son of William Dean's partner. In the social climate of the time and place, these alliances were useful indeed.

Banking was then still in its infancy. The medieval belief that it was a sin to lend money on interest had died hard; men and women with cash to spare were used to keeping it secretly in a chest at home. But when early in the 18th century Parliament legalised charging interest on money loans, banking began to grow, though slowly at first. Only 12 banks were known to exist in England by 1750 and by 1797 there were but 250; yet by the turn of the century 30 flourished in the county of Hampshire alone, with a total of 85 partners providing the capital lent to borrowers in the form of the banks' own paper money.

Normally, the Christchurch, Wimborne & Ringwood Bank would have charged interest of four to five per cent to farmers and graziers for loans for land improvement and drainage, perhaps one half per cent more to dealers in agricultural produce; but to smugglers one can imagine the rate being around 25 per cent for money to purchase contraband goods in France. Few secret sources of clients' income can have remained unknown to a county bank at the time. William Dean especially, owing to his centuries-old family background, would have acquired great knowledge of the material circumstances and financial affairs of the productive folk in the county communities, for whom money was the catalyst of enterprise and trade. When reasonable security was offered they were able to negotiate

This pound note, number 13,303, was issued in 1825 by the Christchurch and Wimborne Bank before it failed in 1827. The name of the bank formerly included Ringwood.

loans with promptitude, and so, at this time of agricultural expansion, the bank prospered.

Only to a limited extent were depositors protected at this time. As a bank of circulation, the Christchurch, Wimborne & Ringwood Bank, like all such banks then, issued its own notes, payable on demand in coinage of the realm, but from 1808 onwards, every bank issuing its own paper money required a licence, granted after proof that it possessed the bullion necessary to redeem a high proportion of it. During the seven years from 1809 to 1816, a total of 143 banks out of the 740 country banks failed to redeem their notes in coin of the realm, and had to cease trading, but the Christchurch, Wimborne & Ringwood Bank remained prosperous.

At the turn of the century, events of great significance for this neglected region of the country loomed on the horizon, events that were to work greatly to William Dean's advantage, multiply his fortune and release forces that would in time change the region's character dramatically.

CHAPTER 3

The Enclosures

SO WILLIAM DEAN put his surgical instruments aside for good in the year 1800 and turned entirely to banking and property transactions, a decision that coincided with a local development of far-reaching importance affecting not only agriculture, but in due course the region's whole character. It was the proposed enclosure of Poole Heath, the lonely region that extended east to west from Christchurch to Poole, and nearly as far as Dorchester, an area covering some 20 square miles, variously described as 'a wilderness' — 'a desolate heath' — 'an unreclaimed solitude'. For on the site of what is now the bustling town of Bournemouth, there were at the start of the 19th century few acceptable houses. 'Forty years ago,' commented the guide book to the infant town, published in 1840, 'two or three mud hovels and a decoy pond, which had been made here owing to the profound stillness of the place, were all that graced the now magnificent Valley . . .'

The heath was then mostly common land good for little but poor grazing and turf cutting for use as domestic fuel. Scraggy cattle and a few sheep nibbled at the sparse herbage, pathetic possessions of a handful of local cottagers. What roads or tracks there were led only to Christchurch and to Poole, from Corfe Mullen, Wimborne, Longham and Wareham, while ruts carved by wagons carrying the turf served also as paths to the sea.

But the thousands of acres of Poole Heath, clothed in purple heather from which legions of bees produced harvests of honey, were now to be thrust from their centuries-old solitude into the ambitious 19th century through the proposed enclosure.

Enclosure of commonly owned lands had, of course, already been undertaken for two or three centuries, as a means of increasing food production. Since the open field system had been recognised as uneconomical, little by little the wide-open stretches of land cut into numerous strips divided by green banks were enclosed, like the uncultivated heaths, and replaced by hedged-off fields for sowing and pasture, assembled into individually owned compact farms. Prompted by ambitious landowners and farmers, 1,475 enclosures were authorised from 1740 to 1799 in separate Acts by Parliament. Objections from humbler folk to the enclosures were normally over-ruled by the commissioners appointed to undertake them, and their decisions had legal force. They were, however, authorised conditionally to compensate with money or land anyone able to show that his land rights, whether established by legal deed or long-held common usage, had been violated, although in practice it did not always occur.

In 1801, increased food production being an urgent need owing to the wars with France, a general Enclosure Act (41 Geo. III chap. 109) under which private enclosures nation-wide were able to be authorised, came into force and cleared the way for more than another hundred of them throughout the country.

Historians have debated interminably about the justice or lack of it, and the social results of enclosure; this account is not the place for a re-statement of them, but the main facts are decisive in the history of the Dean family and the birth of Bournemouth. These are, that the new system of farming enclosed fields certainly yielded greater crops and added to national prosperity for a time. For landowners, large and small, like the Deans and the Dales the potential gains were great, holdings of around £10,000 value in money of the day becoming not uncommon as a result; but the very smallest tenant farmers lost their all, as did labourers who possessed nothing but commoners' rights enabling them to keep a cow or two and a pig with which to ensure their existence. Nation-wide, these men and their families usually become a dispossessed rural proletariat, a charge on the ratepayers.

How did the enclosure of Poole Heath operate? The General Enclosure Act naturally prompted local landowners — the

Earl of Malmesbury, Sir George Ivison Tapps, who was Lord of the Manor, and William Dean — to secure the enclosure of the Heath and for this purpose two separate Acts were in due course passed by Parliament. These were the Canford Enclosure Act, covering areas in Dorset, and the Christchurch Enclosure Act, 1802 (42, George III) — 'an Act for dividing, allotting and enclosing certain commonable lands and waste grounds within the Parish of Christchurch, and the Parish or Chapelry of Holdenhurst, in the County of Southampton'.

The Lord of the Manor of Westover, Sir George Tapps, owned the lands of the Liberty of Westover, but his ownership was not absolute, for the law relating to common land granted tenants with 40 years' occupation rights the use of the heath land; some cottagers, lacking even these rights, were still granted them through custom.

Inevitably, these poor semi-literate cottagers, mainly turf-cutters and vendors, had not the money to hire an attorney to represent their interests. Startled to hear of the proposed enclosures, which they felt to be a threat to their rights, they were beset by a wave of fear and hostility and began disputing as to how they could protect themselves. Their views ranged from a peaceful petition to outright violence.

Three commissioners had meanwhile been appointed to apply the requirements of the Act in Holdenhurst parish. The Earl of Malmesbury, Sir George Tapps and William Dean were unsuitable because of their ownership of land there, but Dean's son-in-law, William Clapcott, was nominated. The other two commissioners were Richard Richardson, a barrister, of Lincoln's Inn Fields, and John Wickens, of Mapperton, Dorset. William Clapcott had joined William Dean's bank a year or two earlier and had married Mary, one of his three daughters, although the date of the marriage is not recorded in the county records. He is believed to have built for himself and his wife The New House at Holdenhurst, an attractive grey stone building still to be seen to the north of the Green.

Each of the commissioners had to swear to 'perform the several trusts, powers and authorities reposed in me as a Commissioner without favour or affection, prejudice or partiality to any person or persons whomsoever ... And I do swear that I will faithfully, impartially and honestly according to the best of

William Clapcott, who married William Dean's daughter Mary, was born in this cottage in Holdenhurst parish about 1770. He joined with disastrous results the bank his father-in-law had established.

my skill and ability, divide, set out and allott certain common-able lands and waste grounds in the parish of Christchurch and parish and Chapelry of Holdenhurst in the County of Southampton according to equity and good conscience'.

Their duties also included making highways and roads, the sale of land to defray expenses and the award of land, as freehold, to approved claimants in compensation for loss of

common or other rights. Thus, the Christchurch Enclosure Act, whatever the final results, does appear on the face of it to try to safeguard the rights of even the humblest people whom its radius of action was due to affect.

The Holdenhurst cottagers with ancient rights on the Heath had meanwhile agreed to do all they could to try to uphold them, and knowing that a local farmer, William West, of Muscliff Farm, had spoken sympathetically of their possible plight, decided to send a deputation to try to enlist his aid.

One summer evening in 1802 the deputation of ragged turf cutters and poor graziers marched through Holdenhurst to

Muscliff, gathering numerous sympathisers on the way, until they arrived at William West's large thatched farmhouse, where the date 1729 was carved above the door, and asked to see him. Aware that the (anti-)Combination Laws of 1800 imposed penalties of imprisonment on workers who assembled with the object of strikes or improving their conditions, and perhaps alarmed at their sudden arrival, William West rebuked them for 'assembling so tumultuously'. However, hearing of their fears for their loss of livelihood, and seeing their agitated state of mind, he agreed to help them and promised to draw up a petition for the allottment of enough of the heath land to provide turf for all those people who had hitherto received it.

Some weeks later, shuffling into the hall where the commissioners were holding their hearings, the cottagers presented their petition and forcefully stated their case. They were heard favourably, but there was no certainty that they would succeed and they waited anxiously.

The enclosure commissioners finished their entire task three years' later in 1805, and recorded it on 91 parchment pages each measuring 28 by 24 inches, with a blue revenue stamp on the top inner margin of every page, and their signatures on the bottom right hand corner. Bound in brown leather and weighing 40 pounds, the volume was entitled 'Commissioners' Award 1805 — West Stour — Hurn-Winkton and Hinton'. It is now deposited in the Town Clerk's strong-room, Bournemouth, an impressive monument to their three years' patient and unremitting labour, but a copy made at the time may be seen in the County Archives at Winchester.

The commissioners had treated the petitioning cottagers generously, granting them, thanks perhaps to the persuasion of William West, an area of 425 acres of five plots to be placed in trust with the Lord of the Manor 'in lieu of their Rights or pretended Rights or customs of cutting turves'. The allotments applied to 'the Occupiers for the time being of all such Cottages and Tenements containing less than one acre each as were erected on ancient sites or were ... erected more than 14 years...

Trying hard to be fair and reasonable, the commissioners said in legalistic phraseology that they 'thought it proper for a Turf Common not exceeding in the whole five acres or less than two acres for each Cottage or Tenement ... in their judgement fit and proper for supplying Turves for Fuel for the use of such Cottages or Tenements and which Allotments ... are forever afterwards to be managed and the Turf arising therefrom to be cut taken and used by the Occupiers ... but such Turf Common shall not be fed or depastured by any Cattle or Sheep ...'

The tenants of the Holdenhurst cottages included Richard Troke, Widow Cole, William Budden, Mary Troke, Benjamin Bugden and Joseph Dyott. Four of these cottages were owned by William Dean. The Holdenhurst turf-cutting allotment, described as containing 147 acres and two roods, was situated at Longmans bottom and bounded by Allotments to the Earl of Malmesbury, John Woodridge, and William Dean respectively; then 'by an Allotment for gravel pits by the Road leading from Great Dean towards Bourn Mouth, and by Allotments to John French, Henry Jenkins and Cornelius Trim respectively'.

The following table provides a useful summary of the Allotment numbers, their purposes and the acreage involved:

Allotment Nos.	Purpose of Allotments	Area A. R. P.
1-24a	Roads	78 0 33
25-29	Gravel for Roads	15 0 7
30	Clay for new Owners & Occupiers	1 2 0
31-57	Sold to 7 Purchasers for £4,100-14-11	1,258 1 1
58-62	In trust to provide turf for fuel	425 0 0
63-71	In lieu of Tithe (Lord Malmesbury)	316 0 35
72-77	Compensation for Interest in the Soil (Sir G.I. Tapps)	240 1 3
78-238	Compensation for loss of common rights (41 persons)	2,749 3 10
		5,084 1 9

In the Liberty of Westover the commissioners made 241 awards, or allotments for private and public ownership, totalling 5,083 acres. These together, it is worth noting, constituted the area of most of the future town of Bournemouth. Roads were their first concern, referred to as 'Public Carriage Roads and Highways, Private Roads, Bridle Ways and Footways', the width and object of each one being stated.

The commissioners were faced at once with decisions far-reaching in their consequences: whether to disregard the age-old tracks across the Heath and impose new roads based upon surveys of the most direct and practicable routes linking various places; or to base new roads on ancient tracks. Sensibly, they chose the latter, thereby saving themselves much work and gaining local approval.

Allotment No.1, the road from Christchurch to Poole, 40 feet wide, they named the Poole Road, now the Christchurch Road, Old Christchurch Road and Poole Road; No.2, from Great Dean to Bourne Mouth, became Holdenhurst Road, 40 feet wide and Bath Road, 30 feet wide; No.3, Charminster to Decoy Pond Lane, 40 feet wide, now Charminster Road; No.4, Muscliff to Decoy Pond Lane, 40 feet wide, the present Wimborne Road; No.5, Redhill to Coomb Corner, 40 feet wide then, now simply a footpath through Redhill Park; No.6, from Poole Road to Boscomb Chine 30 feet wide, now Sea Road; No.7, Decoy Pond Cottage to Bourne Mouth, now Exeter Road. Minor roads, lanes and footpaths made up the

Allotment Nos.	Purchaser	Area A. R. P.
31-35	Sir G.I. Tapps	205 0 22
36	Earl of Malmesbury	2 1 20
37-39	Earl of Malmesbury	57 2 8
40-43	William Driver	153 1 7
44	William Driver	83 0 34
45	Arthur Quartley	21 2 3
46-47	Cornelius Trim	82 0 30
48-53	William Dean	500 0 17
54-56	Philip Norris	141 2 2
57	Philip Norris	11 1 18
		1,258 1 1

other 14 Allotments for roads and included 'from Charminster Road to William Domonie's Cottage'; 'the road in Throop and along old Meadows', described as 'Branching out of an ancient lane called Bury Lane' and another described as 'from the last Road to the Bunny'.

The building of houses several decades later was to change the minor roads and lanes into those streets and residential areas that crystallised into districts of Bournemouth. Described as 'roads' by the commissioners, they were to remain roads in theory for some 50 years before they were macadamised, although with foresight the commissioners set aside Allotments 25-29, some 15 acres, for the Surveyor of Roads and Highways to provide gravel for road repairs. Rational as ever, they even assigned Allotment No. 30, an acre, for clay for the use of house builders.

The terms of the Act obliged the commissioners to cover the costs of their three years' work by the sale of newly enclosed land. With commendable foresight they chose to sell through public auctions — or by private treaty — mainly land with uninterrupted views of the sea, these being assumed to be the most desirable. The table below, which holds one or two surprises, gives the names of the purchasers, with the sums they paid for the areas of land they bought:

	Price Paid £ s. d.	Approximate Situation
	1,050 2 10	South and East Cliffs
	63 10 0	Iford
	296 5 6	Moordown & Stouden
	622 0 6	Redhill & Meyrick Park
	265 2 4	Meyrick Park
	134 9 9	Near Stokewood Road
	378 1 2	Charminster
	639 1 2	West Cliff & King's Park
	599 11 7	Boscombe
	52 10 0	Strouden
	4,100 14 11	

William Dean thus emerged as the major buyer, having with his usual acumen secured perhaps by private treaty 500 acres of the West Cliff and the central area that later became known as Dean Park for £639. This brilliant exploit, or far-sighted acquisition, laid the entire foundation of the Dean family fortune. The other buyers fared less well.

Sir George Tapps, Lord of the Manor, paid £1,050 2s 10d for his 205 acres, about half as much land made up of five plots on the south and east cliff, reaching from William Dean's land to nearly half the distance between the Bourne mouth and Boscombe. William Driver, from Surry Square in the London Borough of Southwark, possibly a land speculator, paid highly for his 236½ acres, comprising 153 acres 1 rood 7 perches at Redhill and Meyrick Park, with another 83 acres 30 perches at Meyrick Park. Philip Norris, who resided at nearby Boscombe Cottage, purchased four plots totalling 141½ acres, but exchanged a plot of about 11 acres costing £52 10s with the Earl of Malmesbury in return for cancellation of tithes due to him.

Lord Malmesbury's four plots, totalling a little less than 60 acres cost him £359 15s 6d, again a high price. Dr Arthur Quartley, a physician residing in Castle Street, Christchurch, who later joined William Dean's Christchurch, Wimborne & Ringwood Bank as a partner, bought just one plot of 21½ acres, near the present-day Stoke Wood Road, and for this he paid £134 9s 9d. Cornelius Trim, a business associate of William Dean, living in Holdenhurst, bought about 82 acres made up of two plots, one of just over 11 acres at Muckleshell and the other of 70 acres 2 roods at Throop, for which he paid £378 1s 3d.

Apart from these plots which they purchased, the local landowners were in addition awarded land as compensation for loss of tithes, loss of rights and interest in the soil, and loss of common rights. Lord Malmesbury, owner of all tithes due on land contained in the Liberty of Westover, was awarded nine plots amounting to about 316 acres in lieu of tithes on the enclosed land. This award contained the district which later came to be described as Malmesbury Park. Sir George Tapps, Lord of the Manor, received six plots of land totalling 240¼ acres between Boscombe and the Lansdowne, next to the plots he had purchased, amounting to much of the land in the area that was to become the town of Bournemouth between Boscombe to Poole Hill road and the sea.

A further 164 awards, the remainder of the Enclosures, amounting to 2,748½ acres, were then distributed between 41 people — 'owners, proprietors, lessees and customary tenants' — 'in proportion to their several and respective Lands, Common Rights, and all other Rights whatsoever in over and upon' the enclosed land 'in full bar of and compensation for all Rights' as a result of the Enclosures.

So two local landowners alone, received together nearly half the total of land distributed in this category. They were, the Lord of the Manor, Sir George Tapps, 704¼ acres, and William Dean, 636½ acres. Added to the 500 acres William Dean had purchased, it brought his total to 1,137 acres, just 12 acres less than that of the Lord of the Manor, and potentially a huge fortune. Thus, had this son of the old Holdenhurst yeoman risen in the world.

The other main beneficiaries in this category were: Cornelius Trim, 201¾ acres, Dr William Farr, 131¾ acres, Richard Dale, 130¾ acres as well as 45 acres jointly with his kinsman William Dean, and another 20¼ acres as trustee for William and Robert Daw, minors; the Reverend George Tito Brice, 218¾ acres, the 'Owners of Moredown Farm', 87¼ acres, Ambrose Daw, 87 acres, John Sloman, 80¾ acres. *(See table overleaf for total land holdings)*:

Finally, an unnumbered award gave to John Cook, in consideration of his former right of common in Week Marsh 'the Right of Common of Pasture for five beasts to go and feed in Week Marsh aforesaid at such times in every year as the said Marsh hath heretofore usually of Right been fed and depastured *(sic)* in common'.

Certain obligations accompanied each allotment. The commissioners gave detailed instructions to the new proprietors to fence before 1st May 1805 the boundaries of their land where they adjoined main roads; and before 1st May 1807 all their other boundaries, with ditches and banks at least five foot six inches high or 'other good and sufficient fences', and such fences 'forever afterwards shall be well and sufficiently maintained supported and kept in repair by the said Proprietors and

Name	Purchased A. R. P.	Interest in Soil A. R. P.	Tithe A. R. P.	Common Rights A. R. P.	Total A. R. P.
Sir G.I.Tapps	205 0 22	240 1 3		704 1 9	1,149 2 34
William Dean	500 0 17			636 3 37	1,137 0 14
Earl of Malmesbury	59 3 28		316 0 35	33 0 5	409 0 28
Cornelius Trim	82 0 30			201 3 13	284 0 3
William Driver	236 2 1				236 2 1
Philip Norris	152 3 20			14 2 35	167 2 15
William Farr				131 3 25	131 3 25
Richard Dale				130 3 39	130 3 39
Rev. George Tito Brice				128 3 17	128 3 17
Owners of Moredown Farm				87 2 17	87 2 17
Ambrose Daw				87 0 29	87 0 29
John Sloman				80 3 5	80 3 5

the future Owners'. They gave additional orders as to the management of waste grounds 'not thought fit to be enclosed' and the care of stock in the former commonable meadows. They also granted powers to the new owners to exchange lands should they wish to do so.

A formidable task was completed. The three commissioners, William Clapcott, Richard Richardson and John Wickens had surveyed in detail the impressive total of 5083 acres 31 perches, listened to the pleas of hundreds of interested parties, relieved with justice the fears for their futures of many humble people, conferred on the privileged the blessings of land whose value in the future would place them among the wealthiest in the land — all in the remarkably short time of three years, without computers or calculators and nothing more formidable than quill pens. They then returned to their own daily occupations, doubtless with an eye over their shoulders to watch the outcome. In the sense that allowing for the political and social climate of the day they could have done only that which they did, it was a formidable achievement.

Three landowners now held in their hands the destiny of the parish of Holdenhurst: they were Sir George Tapps, with 1,149 acres, William Dean, 1,137 acres and the Earl of Malmesbury, 409 acres. All three owned additional lands; Sir George Tapps, the estates of the Manor of Christchurch, the Earl of Malmesbury the Heron Court (now Hurn Court) estate and William Dean the Littledown House estate, increased to about 120 acres in the early 19th century. In addition, ten years before his death in 1794, William Dean's father, John Dean, 'by consideration of the natural love and affection which he hath and beareth for his son', had transferred to him various lands and cottages in Holdenhurst, and in 1787 had also sold him for £926 various other cottages with land in Muckleshell. In a few years, William Dean had become one of the region's two major landowners.

The possession of this land, with no restrictions as to development, is the stuff of which today many men's wildest dreams are made, but there is, of course, no parallel between then and now. Unused land was then abundant, the lone and level fields stretched far away, no planning acts to control building development existed, men built in the style of the day with regard for the feelings of the community in which they lived and worked. Neither the Earl of Malmesbury, nor Sir George Tapps nor William Dean seem to have had any intention of building; for no reason to do so existed on that desolate heath. They were content to carry out the object of the Enclosure Act, that is, to lease the land for ploughing, sowing for cereals and for the creation of good pasture for cattle.

William Dean, and his son-in-law, William Clapcott, were then busy with the Christchurch, Wimborne & Ringwood Bank's affairs, notably the increase in loans for land improvement, drainage and fencing following the enclosures. In any case, William Dean's instincts prompted him to keep any land he had acquired.

Smugglers frequented this once lonely wayside inn, isolated on a bleak stretch of the old road from Christchurch to Poole. Originally named the Tapps Arms after local Lord of the Manor, Sir George Tapps, it was pulled down later, rebuilt and called The Tregonwell Arms, after Lewis Tregonwell.

So, for some years little occurred to disturb the calm of the great heath. The smugglers prospered, some of the enclosed land was put to the plough, planted with wheat, barley and corn or given over to sheep. Evidently, in this first decade of the 19th century, Sir George Tapps began to beautify parts of his land by planting the pine trees that made the region so appealing. William Dean followed suit, until years later from Bourne Mouth to Mount Misery, from the area in the west subsequently called Talbot Woods to Haddons Hill in the north, flourished a semi-circle of young pines, which would change the character of the area in time and give to Bournemouth its unique character and reputation as a health resort.

The only building, so far as can be ascertained, during this first decade, was a wayside inn, near to where the Bourne river crossed the main road and the junction of what are now Post Office Road and Old Christchurch Road. Shown in later photographs as a double-fronted white stucco house roofed with grey slates, it was named The Tapps Arms. In those days, when giant breweries supplying the entire needs of their tied houses were unknown, the first landlord would no doubt have brewed his ale from water drawn from his own well. Travellers and smugglers frequented the house and it gained fame as a wayside place of resort for clandestine assignations.

It was to this inn, in the days when William Dean and his partners were living well on the proceeds of their flourishing bank, that there came on 14 July 1810 one Lewis Tregonwell, Esquire, former sheriff of Dorset, who had driven over in his horse-drawn carriage from the nearby small resort of Muddiford, or Mudeford as it is now called.

His visit started a chain of events that were to change the whole character of the region and lead in due course to the birth and growth of Bournemouth. What then, happened? The Hon. Grantley Berkeley, a famous *bon viveur* of the time, gives his own fanciful version of the events in his autobiography, *Life and Recollections,* and while it strays markedly from historic fact, in so far as the trees planted were pine, not fir, it is entertaining enough to read in full. 'It's an odd place, and of strange history,' he begins.

Listen: I knew it when it was in its wild state of heather, and its name was only known from the juncture of the little rivulet of Bourne, at that particular spot, with the sea. On a dark night, a lord of the soil drove up in his carriage, and, halting on a slight eminence, he exclaimed to his steward, 'How far am I from the sea?'

'Close, sir,' was the reply; 'you will hear the surf if you listen.'

'Good,' said the great man, 'let there be houses here; and mind, as people at watering places love shaded and sequestered spots, plant — plant, sir, well with the Scotch fir — fir, d'ye mind me, nothing else will grow.'

'Where shall we plant, sir?'

'Here, here,' said the great man, waving his hand in the murky air, and turning round till he forgot his position as regarded the whereabouts of the vasty deep, and ordered the trees to be planted in front of the row of houses.

The lord of the soil who commanded this was a gentleman of the old school, of a warm heart and an open hand, and one whom to know was but to like; his word was a law against which there was no appeal, so his steward obeyed him to the letter.

House upon house, no two of them at all alike, soon reared their walls over the dreary heather, till the village or watering place assumed the likeness of a Chinese puzzle . . . The houses had scarce been raised by their proprietors before wise men were found to take them; an inn was built, baths sprang up, bathing machines of different patterns spotted the beach, fat women were found to attend them, and there was nothing wanted but a parson, a butcher, a baker, and an hostler; the doctor and the lawyer were regarded as sure to follow of their own free will, as Satan may be supposed finally to attend a congregation of sinners.

This then, was Mr Berkeley's version of the birth of Bournemouth. What did occur was rather different but even more appealing.

CHAPTER 4

Hard Times

THE VALLEY OF the Bourne would probably have continued to slumber undisturbed for another half century, its calm broken only by the cry of seagulls and the laughter of the sea bathers who now and then splashed about in the water — but for the visit of Lewis Tregonwell and his wife in July, 1810. They had driven over from the nearby resort of Mudeford, to stay at the Tapps Arms, walk by the lovely beach or to indulge cautiously in a little sea-bathing.

After a century or more of disrepute, sea-bathing had become fashionable, given impetus through a learned treatise published by a Dr Russell, who declared sea water to be nature's great rejuvenator for men and women of all ages. Clad in black or navy-blue costumes designed to hide their bodies, bathers stepped gingerly into the water and splashed around until they felt renewed. Royal approval had coloured this panacea. At Weymouth in 1789, King George III descended the hooded steps of his bathing machine (those tiny cabins on wheels) and bravely took the plunge while nearby on the sands the Dorset Rangers' brass band played with enthusiasm — 'God save great George, our king'! A prayer which was answered, for the king survived his dip.

It was perhaps a less glorious, but certainly more fateful occasion 30 years later, when sad Mrs Tregonwell, moved by the peace and beauty of the place — its little river winding down to the sea through the purple heather — told her husband how agreeable it would be to build a house and live there. Lewis Tregonwell was delighted, for since the death of their infant son, Grosvenor, two years earlier, his wife, grief-stricken, could interest herself in nothing. Thinking that the sea air had wrought its cure on her he readily agreed to her wish, and in due course advised the owner of the land, Sir George Tapps, with whom he was acquainted, of his desire to purchase a plot there. Since Sir George had no objections to selling what appeared to be a fairly worthless piece of heathland, negotiations were concluded for Lot 31 in the Enclosure Award. In the title deeds of the plot, dated 25 September 1810, it is described as 'all that piece or parcel of common land or heath situate, lying, being at or near Bourn in the Parish of Holdenhurst, containing by estimation eight acres and two roods and eight perches . . . bounded by a footpath or way leading from the Decoy and Cottage by the Decoy Enclosures on the east, by a public carriage way leading from the said Decoy Cottage, to the sea on the west . . .'

The agreement having been signed, Lewis Tregonwell paid Sir George the sum of £179 11s. 0d. in 'lawful English money' and upon his 8 acres of heathland built the large country house there called 'the Mansion', later known as Exeter House, and now part of the Royal Exeter hotel. For his butler, Symes, he also had built in the grounds of his prestigious dwelling an attractive little thatched cottage. The venture was a success. Taking up residence in their new home in April 1812, so happily did the Tregonwells live there in the summer season that they decided to share their pleasure with people of similar tastes and resources.

Sir George Tapps favoured their plan and in 1814 sold Lewis Tregonwell more land, this time at £40 an acre, nearly twice the price of his first purchase. On this newly acquired land, more houses of impressively large size and assorted styles were built a few years later. For this reason Lewis Tregonwell has been called, perhaps not very accurately, the 'founder of Bournemouth'. He was certainly the first resident-proprietor.

While the Tregonwells were enjoying their new home in 1812, an event occurred that was to put a brake upon the development of Bourne Mouth — and the Dean estates — for nearly 40 years. It was the death on 16 November 1812 of William Dean, buried in the newly-built grand family vault in Holdenhurst churchyard which can still be seen today in the shadow of the Victorian church. Last of the male line of the predominant Holdenhurst yeomen, he was as we know, the owner at the time of his death of key estates amounting to nearly 1,200 acres in the region of Bourne Mouth, as it was then called.

But far from ending his power and influence over his estates, William Dean's death was to increase it, for in 1809 he had made a will that would so tie his family's hands that for the next 40 years life would become something of a burden for them. The will shows clearly that contrary to what has since been published, he had no wish for his land to be sold for residential building; in fact, the terms of his will prevented it. With his friends Sir George Henry Rose, former treasurer of the Navy, George Rose and James Topp, as trustees, he established a trust that entailed his estate first to his son or daughter then to their children and their children's children. (To each of his trustees he bequeathed among other generous benefits a mourning ring made of jet with a diamond inserted.)

The trust covered all 'the manors and freehold messuages lands tenements and hereditaments whatsoever situate . . . in Holdenhurst and in the parish of Christchurch Twyneham and elsewhere in England . . . subject to the right of dower of testator's wife Mary Dean'.

To his daughter, Mary Clapcott, he gave absolutely all his farm animals and crops, and the rents and profits of the properties on his estate to be delivered to her half-yearly; to her husband, William Clapcott, he bequeathed the use for life of Littledown House, its grounds and cottages as well as numerous other properties and lands in the trust. Should William and Mary Clapcott have neither sons nor daughters — and when the will was made they had not — the properties were to be held on trust under the same conditions for William Dean's cousin Richard Dean, and after him his children. Thus, the trust in effect prohibited the transformation of farm and heath land into residential property.

In his old age, William Dean opposed change. For example, the trustees were empowered to dispose of trust land only for the purpose of investing in other agricultural land. And after payment of his legacies and any debts from his residuary estate, they were to invest the balance in stock or securities prior to purchasing even more land.

Seemingly, before his death, he imagined his farms lasting

forever, rich with cattle and furnished with up-to-date agricultural buildings. He left the then substantial sum of £1,000 specifically for such improvements. Proud of his ancient name, he ruled, moreover, that any son or sons of Mary Clapcott who inherited his estate 'should take and bear the surname of Dean and in case of neglect or refusal to do so should forfeit the inheritance in favour of the next person in line'.

Busy as he was, William Dean had acquired a taste for good living, furnishing his house with quality furniture and laying down a cellar of fine wines and liqueurs, all of which he left to his wife. His cousin Richard Dean, was to be offered the lease on nominal terms of Carew's Farm, Holdenhurst, which, of course, he himself had bought some 30 years ago, and in which he had resided until the purchase of Little Down.

Though unable to sell or develop the estates, his heirs were left very well off. But in January 1811, about a year before his death, William Dean added a startling codicil to his will concerning his business as a banker. The trustees had first been empowered either to carry on the business together with his partners, or to discontinue it altogether and wind up his interests in it. But as the months passed and his end approached, William Dean found himself forced to entertain second thoughts.

The first of these two proposals for the bank's future after his death — that his three trustees should together fill his place as senior partner — was fraught with so many obvious difficulties as to be quite impractical. The second, the closure of the bank, which had been operating profitably, was undoubtedly opposed by the two partners, William Castleman, a lawyer, who was also William Dean's legal adviser, and George Adams.

There remained a third alternative, which perhaps for good reasons William Dean had hesitated to put forward earlier. Why not make his son-in-law, William Clapcott, husband of his only child Mary, his successor? But perhaps in view of his

William Clapcott, seen in this portrait of about 1810, by an unknown artist, led the Christchurch, Ringwood and Wimborne Bank from prosperity to bankruptcy. He had gambled with commodities and made loans to the infant states of South America.

relative inexperience and their doubts as to the suitability of his temperament for the role of senior partner with a last word in banking policy, the partners found this, the most obvious solution, hard to accept without some limitations to control the young man's known leanings towards speculation. So, William Dean added this startling codicil to his will: 'Said testator nominated said William Clapcott as his successor in the Banking firm of Dean, Castleman and Adams . . ., and gave him all his share capital and interest', but, he added in clear and emphatic words a warning clause: 'DECLARATION that all his said Estates should be subject to and charged with the payment of all losses which might be incurred in said business. And that the said William Clapcott should repay all such (with interest) as should be occasioned after Testator's death.'

So, it was a double-faced gift that William Clapcott, fornmer commissioner of the Enclosures Act, received on his father-in-law's death. Henceforth, he was responsible not simply for his own share of any losses, but also for all losses which the bank might from now on incur by whatever means, thus freeing the other two partners from all liabilities. Yet such was his nature that he accepted the risk, not realising the havoc this condition was to play in the lives of his wife, himself and their only son, also called William, born in the year his grandfather died.

Unfortunately, by 1818, under six years of William Clapcott's leadership the bank had begun to make heavy losses; and on 10 October of that year William Castleman resigned and withdrew his capital. Henceforward, the bank was called Dean, Clapcott and Adams. It was the beginning of a chapter of financial disasters, in which Castleman seemingly played an unscrupulous role. In dire need of money to meet the bank's liabilities, William Clapcott obtained from him a loan of £2,800, the security being a mortgage at 5 per cent over 60 years of the property inherited from William Dean in which he and his wife had a life interest.

It was not enough, for William Clapcott's and George Adam's loss-making direction of the bank gradually forced them into a succession of such loans. In December 1820, William Clapcott borrowed £1,200 from Castleman on the same security as before; in 1826 he turned to Castleman for another

£3,900. For this, Castleman obtained as security all the freehold farms and other property which the trustees had purchased out of the surplus of William Dean's residual estate, as well as the income from the residue of his personal estate not yet invested, plus also a 1,000-year-lease on 50 acres of land given under the Enclosure Award to William Dean.

William and Mary Clapcott now owed William Castleman the very large sum then of £7,900, and Castleman's exactions for this were severe. Not only did he receive interest at the then highest rate, five per cent per annum, but in addition, the income in kind and cash from Mary Clapcott's inherited properties and securities, which were of much greater value than the money he had advanced. Yet this same William Castleman was the family's legal adviser, as was his son, Edward Castleman, on his father's death. Harsh though his terms were, Castleman may cynically have justified himself on the grounds that he was using them as a weapon to deter William Clapcott from ruinous speculation in what was at the time a dangerous field.

For the 1820s brought in a highly speculative trend in banking circles, leading to a panic and crisis in 1825 with the failure of a prominent London bank, Pole & Company, owing £300,000 in money of the day, a disaster that also hit numerous country banks. The main causes were short-term loans to South American governments, which were not repaid; investment in speculative mining ventures in South America, which generally showed losses and heavy speculation in commodities, surely the road to ruin.

So dangerous did the financial situation then become that the Bank of England advanced £300,000 to Pole & Company to prevent its bankruptcy, while at the same time meeting demands for payment in gold sovereigns for millions of pounds of paper money. Night and day, the mint worked producing sovereigns, and at one time the Bank of England held reserves of only £1,300,000 of bullion. But by the year's end faith in the banking system returned, the panic subsided and normal conditions began.

This, then, was the financial background to William Clapcott's banking losses, and there is little doubt that he trod the same speculative road as others in the banking community. His losses, however, did not stop, but continued to grow, so that in 1827 he turned to the ever-ready Castleman for a loan of another £2,500, making a total then of £10,400 in money of the day.

And Castleman inevitably increased still more his hold upon the Dean Estates. William Dean's wife, Mary, had died in 1826, joining him in the family vault in Holdenhurst churchyard, having left her daughter, Mary Clapcott, a life interest in all her freehold properties, authorising her at the same time to decide who should receive these life interests upon her death. William Castleman, who, it should be remembered, was also Mary Clapcott's legal adviser, now had himself named as the person to whom these life interests should be bequeathed; and at the same time, to give him even greater security for the £10,400 loan, Mary Clapcott was obliged to mortgage with him additional property she owned in the nearby hamlet of Muckleshell. In case of default in repayments of principal and interest, it was agreed that William Castleman was authorised to sell first, the property mortgaged by William Clapcott and then, if need be, also that mortgaged by his wife.

To make matters worse, William Clapcott's partner, George Adams, died in October 1825, his wife Sarah then taking his place for a year, after which she quickly resigned. She was succeeded by Dr Arthur Quartley, a physician and former mayor of Christchurch, the firm becoming known as Clapcott, Quartley and Company. It was a last desperate effort by William Clapcott to keep solvent, but it failed. In March 1826, the bank that William Deam founded had to stop trading. William Clapcott and the unfortunate Dr Quartley were able to pay some, but not all of the bank's debts out of a large sum of money owed to it by George Adams, and paid out of his estate. But the £10,400 owned by him personally to William Castleman remained outstanding.

In November 1827, Castleman pressed for payment. Unable to find the money, William Clapcott looked desparingly around for someone to take on the mortgage, pay off Castleman and prevent the seizure of the properties by him. Samuel Bignold, a Norwich banker and lawyer, also Chairman of Norwich Union Insurance, thought he saw profit in the transaction, and agreed. In return for a transfer to him of the mortgaged property, with all the rents due from them, he agreed to a new mortgage for £10,000 in November 1827, with interest at five per cent; and thus Castleman got his money.

William Clapcott was now simply playing for time in the expectation that something would turn up to relieve him of his problems, and soon it did, though not quite in the way that he had hoped.

Meantime, it had become clear to Sir George Henry Rose and other trustees that under the terms of William Dean's will they themselves might now become personally liable for the bank's losses, since these were chargeable to his personal estate. They decided to protect themselves. In return for a cash payment of £2,500 towards the still uncleared debts of the defunct bank, William Clapcott and Dr Quartley agreed 'so far as they lawfully could to release the real and residuary personal estates of William Dean from all claims in respect of such debts or losses . . .'

Life for William and Mary Clapcott at this time would have been a crushing burden. They had to endure the painful and ironic predicament of living in a fine mansion, owning some 1,400 acres with numerous cottages and farmhouses, while having barely enough money upon which to live and pay the estate workers — all because of mortgage payments which left them with no ready money. And on 26 April 1831, William Clapcott was forced once again to go cap-in-hand to Samuel Bignold for a further loan of £3,100, making a total of £13,500.

The anxiety and bitterness, the vexation of spirit, the sense of living in chains from which he could not escape, all became too much for William Clapcott. The relief from his troubles he had hoped for now came. On 26 July 1833, two years after his last borrowing from Bignold, he died at the age of 64, leaving his wife Mary and his only son and namesake William, a tall, black-bearded, but very shy young man of 21, to cope as best they could with their very alarming financial predicament.

His death oddly enough became a turning point in the family history. Mary Clapcott, then aged 61, had inherited something of the fighting spirit shown by her father and grandfather. Also, having a better head for business than her husband, she began to try to restore the family fortunes. First, she decided that the existing mortgages with Samuel Bignold

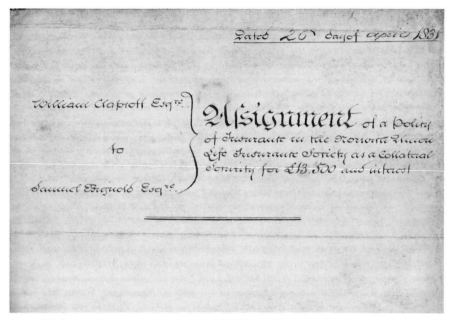

This legal agreement marked William Clapcott's efforts to stave off bankruptcy. He mortgaged the family property with the Norwich Union Insurance Society for the then substantial sum of £13,500, but to no avail.

should, if possible, be re-arranged on more favourable terms with a local banker, William Rolls Fryer, with whom she was acquainted; and, even more importantly, that the Dean estates should be disentailed so as to free them for the kind of development that had begun around the settlement of Bourne Mouth. This disentailment, agreed by the remaining trustees, was completed in the High Court of Chancery on 13 December 1834. William Fryer also agreed to take over the mortgage with Samuel Bignold for £13,500, with his consent, and to advance Mary Clapcott another £1,500 for current expenses. This transaction also took place in December.

Mary Clapcott had so far done well. But her task was helped by the increase in local land values, for while development of the Dean Estates had, by the terms of old William Dean's will, been prevented, building and land values in 'the new romantic watering place called Bourne' (*Hampshire Advertiser*, June 1838) were rising at what the paper termed a 'railway pace' — an impressively modern metaphor based on the new steam locomotives, the fastest things then on earth, puffing through the tranquil English countryside, linking up its far-away places. Lewis Tregonwell had sparked off the increases through his use of the lands he had purchased from Sir George Ivison Tapps.

The Bourne Tregonwell estate comprised land on both sides of what is now Exeter Road, and above the present Cranbourne Road. Here, near his own house, overlooking the road near Prospect (later Terrace) Mount, Lewis Tregonwell had built a cottage for his gardener on a site now occupied by the Hotel Merville. In addition he had purchased from Sir George Ivison Tapps land contained today by Old Christchurch Road, Yelverton Road, Richmond Hill and west of Exeter Road southwards to the 3½-acre South Cliff estate leased to his friend, Mr J.S.W. Erle Drax, who had built a rustic cottage in the wooded grounds.

Northwards, the Tregonwell estate extended to Poole Road (now Commercial Road) and westwards to the Dean estate, which was bounded for more than 10,000 feet in the south by the foreshore. Lewis Tregonwell had purchased his land from Sir George Tapps at prices varying from £20 to £60 an acre. He had also bought the Tapps Arms, which he demolished and had rebuilt as the Tregonwell Arms, the first licensee of which, in 1831, was George Barrow. Later, George Fox bought the inn from Mrs Tregonwell and ran it for 11 years, the last nine as postmaster too — the inn doing duty as the only local post office — until his retirement in 1848. William Fryer occupied Cliff Cottage at one time but later in the 1870s this too was demolished and replaced by two apartment houses. These, joined together, were named Southcliff House, and after many years became the Regent Palace Hotel.

A family succession now spurred on local developments. In March 1835, Sir George Tapps died. He was succeeded as Lord of the Manor of Christchurch by his son, George William Tapps, MP for Christchurch, who assumed the name of Tapps-Gervis, Gervis being a family name. His succession was to prove a powerful stimulus to the development of the 'marine village of Bourne', as people were soon to begin calling it.

The first little local guidebook, published about 1840,

B.Ferrey Arch. M.A.S.L.

*Benjamin Ferrey, the acclaimed Victorian architect who planned
the Pleasure Gardens, made this drawing of the Tregonwell
mansion (left background) about 1840. It is now incorporated in the
Royal Exeter Hotel.*

recalled the event in stately prose. Sir George 'became satisfied', it declared, 'that Bournemouth was endowed by nature
with those special features and circumstances which eminently
fitted it to become an approved resort of those, who, at the ter-
mination of the London season, seek on the coast that invigor-
ating repose, and that commixture of fashion and retirement,
which afford the best protection against *ennui*, and are most
conducive to the restoration of that freshness and activity, both
in the physical and mental functions which the constant excite-
ments of town life have so great a tendency to undermine.'

Day & Haghe Lith:ᵗˢ to the King

Whether John Sydenham, the author of the guide, was simply guessing, or whether Sir George Tapps-Gervis confessed his feelings, we do not know, but clearly, the marine settlement of Bourne was soon to become a very grand place indeed, inhabited by only the very best people, and then for only half the year! To fit the image, Sir George engaged as architect Mr Benjamin Ferrey, a pupil of the much praised Augustus Pugin. His brief was to design the marine village of Bourne on the east side of the little river, every house being detached, shaded by trees, adorned by flowering shrubs, standing in its own generous grounds and costing at least £500, top price for a gentleman's residence.

First to be built were the Westover Villas. Mr David Tuck, a local builder engaged as a general contractor by Sir George,

This water colour of 'Bourne Mouth' by Harriet Daniell, done about 1848, shows the assortment of villas of all shapes and sizes that had mushroomed on land east of the Bourne rivulet, acquired from Sir George Tapps by Lewis Tregonwell.

built the first one. It was offered for sale with an 80 years' lease on 27 March 1837. Nearby, Sir George also had built the Bath Hotel, which was opened to the public on Queen Victoria's Coronation Day, 28 June 1838. It was described in the guide as 'a very elegant, spacious and convenient structure, capable of afffording accommodation to a great number of inmates', under the management of Miss Toomer. Close to the beach arose the Belle Vue Boarding House, fitted 'with every regard to elegance and comfort' for visitors who preferred a 'retired and quiet mode of life'. By the end of 1838, twelve villas of Ferrey's designs, varying with unashamed exuberance from Gothic to Tudor to Italian Renaissance, had been completed by different building speculators on land leased from Sir George. Another four were to follow by 1841.

John Sydenham celebrated these developments in more richly encrusted prose:

Thus, on spots where, before, the foot of man rarely pressed, but the lowly heath flower blossomed and faded in unnoticed solitude, where no sound was heard but the rustling of the rank grass and the wild shrub, as they waved in the light sea-breeze — there a number of detached villas, each marked by distinct and peculiar architectural features, have sprung into existence, affording accommodation of varying extent, so as to be suited to the convenience of either large or small families, and adapted, some for extended, others for confined, establishments. To all these are attached ample gardens, whilst in the front are shrubberies tastefully laid out and walks arranged with due regard to convenience and effect. At one end of this range stands a spacious and commodious hotel, erected for the accommodation of more temporary visitants, and fitted up in the most complete style. All these edifices command views of the ocean, of the distant coast, and of the vale lying immediately beneath, whilst the site is, at the same time, so judiciously chosen, that they are effectually sheltered from the biting winds of the north and east.

Bourne Mouth now grew daily in popularity. The *Hampshire Advertiser* carried an announcement in June 1838 that five 'marine villas' were to be auctioned at the Bath Hotel, all of which were very quickly sold. Soon afterwards 'furnished and papered' villas fitted with 'every requisite' were advertised at four guineas weekly for a monthly rental. The little guide book depicted glowingly the rustic scene that intending visitors saw:

Midway between Christchurch and Poole the road conducts the traveller into a narrow vale opening directly upon the sea shore, and on entering which he is delighted with the prospect of social life, animated retirement and a combination of the elegancies of nature and of art, spread before his view.

Detached villas, indicating every variety of style that the fancy and ingenuity of the architect could devise, admirably associating with the local natural features; rows of stately edifices, relieved by the dark foliage of dense plantations; extensive walks; and tastefully arranged shrubberies, are the objects that first strike the eye in this pleasing retreat; whilst the whole is softened by an air of tranquil repose and a quietude of character eminently grateful to those who seek a relaxation from the fatigue and excitement of fashionable life, or a respite from the turmoils and anxieties of rough intercourse with the world.

This pleasing spot, "Embowered in trees and hardly known to fame", the beauties of which are enhanced by the contrast afforded by the surrounding scenery, is Bournemouth, where, in a season, the magic hand of enterprise has converted the silent and unfrequented vale into the gay resort of fashion and the favoured retreat of the invalid.

Mary Clapcott and her son William watched with interest and frustration these developments that sent land values soaring, but in which the fatal clause in her father's will, as well as her late husband's banking losses and the mortgage of the estates, barred them from sharing. By 1839 the blessings for them in these changes had become too apparent. They realised that the value of their property mortgaged with William Rolls Fryer was far greater than the £15,000 that they owed him.

In April 1839 therefore, Mary Clapcott put to him that six parcels of land amounting to 714 acres, allotted to William Dean under the Enclosures Award, should be released, freed entirely from the mortgage, and returned to her and her son William Clapcott Clapcott, as he was then quaintly called. Evidently, Mary Clapcott knew what she was about, for three of the pieces of land, numbered 48, 50 and 51 on the Award map, though rough heath land, possessed a frontage of several hundred yards along the seashore.

She had chosen well. But would William Fryer agree?

CHAPTER 5

The Marine Village

O N THAT BRIGHT spring morning of 2 May 1839, Mary Clapcott and her son William drove in their carriage and pair through the leafy lanes of Wimborne to meet the banker, William Rolles Fryer, at Lychett House, with what could only have been a sense of triumph. Surprisingly, William Fryer had accepted her proposal for the return of 714 acres of the Dean Estates to her free of mortgage — 'satisfied', he had written, 'that the rest of the property is ample security'. And so that morning she signed the voluminous agreement, three long sheets of vellum in barely legible lawyer's script — for the length of a legal document at that time largely governed what lawyers charged their clients. It is unlikely that she tried to read the whole repetitive thing, relying instead upon the advice of her lawyer, none other than Edward, son of William Castleman. But driving back to Littledown House she would surely have felt happy that she had won back at least a portion of the estates, even though it amounted to only the least valuable part of the lands mortgaged for £15,000 — a mortgage that still cramped and burdened their lives.

Why then, since the estates were disentailed should she not sell the land now released to raise money for their own living expenses? The answer is that this was heath land, some distance away from the developing Bourne estuary area, which nobody would have been willing to buy at that time except at a give-away price, repellent to a person of Mary Clapcott's background. Secondly, she nursed a secret, as we shall see later, a secret not known perhaps even to her son, which would make her at the time absolutely opposed to a sale. She preferred to shoulder the burden of debt.

How was William affected by the anxiety over lack of money amid the trappings of apparent wealth, which had over-shadowed his life for as long as he could remember? Socially, his parents had mixed very little, of necessity, so he had met few of either sex of his own generation. Nor had he any school-fellows, or their sisters as friends, for he been educated at home by ill-paid tutors who rode on their nags up to Little-down House with saddlebags stuffed with books. While his contemporaries made friends far and wide, he languished at home, alone but for his mother, the few estate workers and — the farm animals.

The effects upon him were predictable. Extreme shyness be-came his outstanding characteristic from his early years and stayed with him throughout most of his life, leading later, as we shall see, to eccentricity. His shy and retiring manner little accorded with his impressive looks, his considerable height, burly shoulders and black beard, seemingly belonging to a stronger more forthright character. The stranger would be struck by the contrast between his dominating physical ap-pearance and his almost diffident manner, not knowing that it was born out of a lack of trust of the world caused by the circumstances of his early life.

Compensating perhaps for his lack of human contacts, he developed from boyhood onwards a strong love for animals, especially dogs and horses, not just horses he could ride, but cart-horses, plough horses, even donkeys. When, in due course, more money did become available he bred his own pack of foxhounds and a stable of hunters, which, with his groom, his huntsman and one or two business associates he hunted in the surrounding countryside. In a quiet tree-shaded corner of Littledown House grounds he laid out a tomb for his much-loved dogs. He was terrified of rats, and would avoid any part of the property where had seen any. He employed local lads as rat-catchers and roaring approval, threw handfuls of coins to them from an upstairs window when they held up their catch by their tails. So strong was his phobia that he even wore leather gauntlets to throw out the money.

In 1839, the year that his mother had achieved the agree-ment with William Fryer, releasing the 714 acres, William, then 27, decided that he should marry and beget an heir to inherit the fortune that he hoped would one day be his. Mary Clapcott naturally wished the ancient Dean family to continue and doubtless urged him to do so. Unfortunately, the only eligible young lady he knew at all well was his cousin, Jane Dean, and of her he was reputedly very fond indeed, even in love, although she was three years his senior and already 30 years old. Jane was the second daughter of William's uncle, Richard Dean, a prosperous farmer of Holdenhurst. Her elder sister, Elizabeth, had in 1832 married one Joseph Cooper, who came from the Isle of Wight, and already had two sons by him, of whom we will be hearing more later.

When he began thinking of marriage, William mustered his courage, told Jane of his love for her and his wish to marry her. One can imagine the scene of his proposal — a quiet walk together around the new Holdenhurst church built to replace the old Saxon church in 1834; or a stroll in the orchard of her father's farm, or, a more formal meeting in the farmhouse parlour, surrounded by old oak furniture and Staffordshire china.

Jane evidently was willing, nevertheless nothing came of it. Family opposition was too strong. Jane's sister, Elizabeth, may have stirred it up on the false ground of consanguinity, knowing that if William stayed single, her own sons must inherit his fortune. From a Machiavellian viewpoint, it was a glittering prospect. Her son James, who did inherit years later, said in a letter to solicitor Thomas Rawlins after William's death, that he had 'always understood that the law would not allow them to be married', which, of course, is incorrect. He does not say, however, that Jane opposed it, so we can safely assume that she was for it, yet prevented by this illusory obstacle. Relations between William and the Coopers subsequently grew cold; they left the district. For William and Jane it may not have been the end of the affair, as we shall see, but still a landmark in his life and the Dean history

While direct male descent had ended with Mary Clapcott's father, changing with her to female descent, this line too of the family would now, after the 300 years of which we are aware, become extinct. For Mary Clapcott, who had been struggling to restore the family's fortunes, it was an event touched with sadness. On the other hand, William, after careful reflection probably mused that he was destined for a bachelor's life, and

Mudeford, pictured in this 1861 engraving, rivalled Bournemouth as a seaside resort in the 1850s, but its popularity declined. In a local guidebook it was described as 'an admired spot, the favourite summer residence of numerous families of distinction'.

looked forward to the day when he would have enough money to indulge his own interests — to establish his own stables and kennels, and keep as many animals as possible.

But it was upon the continued growth of the settlement of Bourne Mouth — for this it still was called in the late 1830s — that the rise in land prices depended which would increase the value of the Dean estates; and though it seemed likely, there was no certainty that this would occur. It might follow the discouraging example of nearby Mudeford, lying to the east of the 'mother town' of Christchurch. Since 1803, Mudeford had promised renown as a seaside resort, yet had failed dismally to challenge either Weymouth or Brighton, remaining simply a melancholy little village by the sea. Some years later, it was described by the sportsman and author, Grantley Berkeley, who preferrred it to Bournemouth, as 'an unpretending little place', and, with a teasing note — 'a quiet little village, so retired that when ladies come there, they do not think it necessary in their walks to be followed by a footman caned and cocked-hatted'.

Two or three fortunate events now moved in favour of the Bourne Mouth settlement. First, came the vision and determination of Sir George Tapps-Gervis, who, as we know, engaged Benjamin Ferrey to plan a development scheme for his estates, and took part personally in the management of it, even so far as buying the bricks and the cement. Ferrey's scheme included the Pleasure Gardens design — now the Pine Walk — the Westover Villas, Westover Gardens and plans for several villas of vividly contrasting designs in what was to be called Poole Crescent.

Through a private Act of Parliament, Sir George Tapps-Gervis next obtained authority for further development by trustees until his son came of age, for he was anticipating his own early death. The preamble to the Act declared that a considerable part of the estate was situated upon or near the sea coast at Bourne Mouth and that its situation 'by reason of the salubrity of the air and its proximity to the sea-coast, is well adapted for a watering place'. It went on to say that 'the testator, in his lifetime, with a view to its becoming a fashionable place of resort, granted building leases of certain portions of the said lands and hereditaments, for the erection of detached villas, of which nineteen have been built; and he also expended considerable sums of money in the erection of a hotel for the accommodation of visitors and in the construction of a church...'

At the same time, a Mr William Gordon purchased part of the estate of a Scottish lady, Miss Bruce, which lay west of Wimborne Road and north of Poole Road. William Gordon commissioned an architect named Shepherd to design a number of large, attractive houses which he then had built near what was later to be called Richmond Hill. In contrast to the random building on the Tregonwell estate, Ferrey and Shepherd planned a carefully laid out seaside town. Yet this and other similar developments would have remained only an exercise on paper, but for a well-planned publicity scheme.

It happened as a result of the successful publication of the first volume of a study of English health spas by Dr A.B. Granville. No mere itinerant medico with a literary bent, Italian-born Auguste Bozzi Granville, M.D., Fellow of the Royal Society and holder of various foreign decorations, had published several works on popular watering-places, including *The Spas of Germany, The Mineral Springs of Vichy, Kissingen: Sources & Resources,* and in 1841 the celebrated first volume of *The Spas of England,* which had won acclaim among the wealthier sections of the nation.

A small group of would-be developers of Bourne Mouth were quick to see that he might be of very great help indeed to them if he could be induced to visit and praise the little place, and in an apparently casual way they wrote to him describing the merits of Bourne Mouth, for inclusion in his second volume, inviting him to look in on them should he happen to be passing. Dr Granville agreed to look in, and the visit turned out to be gilt-edged, better even than an invitation to royalty in terms of publicity then and later.

Dr Granville wrote subsequently that, as he happened in February 1841 to be in the neighbourhood of Bourne Mouth, he 'was requested by several gentlemen connected with that almost unknown sea watering place' to come and give his professional assessment of its future. Accommodated in great comfort in one of the Westover Villas allotted exclusively to him and his entourage, where the food and wines were of the best, he spent two or three days studying and assessing Bourne Mouth. He then gave his views in a long after-dinner speech to his hosts at the Bath Hotel, where he had been entertained, he declared, in 'a style of excellence seldom surpassed even in the metropolis'. The splendid hospitality yielded rich dividends, for it had encouraged him to study with even greater care than usual Bourne Mouth's possibilities for development as a watering place. He rose to his feet after his excellent dinner and delivered a speech that was in some ways a paean of praise. It was to appear later in his second published volume of the influential guide to English spas.

'I have examined Bourne in all its parts, under sunshine as well as during the prevalence of wet and high wind,' he declared.

I have no hesitation in stating, as the conclusion of all my observations, around as well as within the place — that no situation that I have had to examine along the whole Southern Coast possesses so many capabilities of being made the very first invalid sea-watering place in England: and not only a watering-place, but what is still more important, a winter residence for the delicate constitutions requiring a warm and sheltered locality at this season of the year...'

Dr Granville saw Bourne Mouth first as a haven for invalids, invalidism for the well-off being then a recognised way of life, and he continued:

I hardly need touch upon its superiority as a bathing-place to any in the neighbourhood, or along these coasts. It is as an inland sheltered haven for the most tender invalids however, that I would call your attention to the great capabilities of Bourne; for we look in vain elsewhere for that singular advantage which Bourne possesses, of presenting two banks of cliffs, clothed with verdure even at this inclement season, running from the sea inland, with a smiling vale, watered by a rapid brook or bourne, dividing them just enough to allow of a most complete ventilation, with coolness in the summer, and yet affording a most protected succession of ridges upon which to erect residences not only for convalescents ... but also for patients in the most delicate state of health as to lungs.'

The worthy doctor's own lungs would have needed to be in robust condition to utter a sentence of such length and complexity, but he managed easily enough and capped it with a warning, eventually disregarded, to his audience about allowing Bourne Mouth to become ugly and commonplace:

You must not let in strangers and brick-and-mortar contractors to build up whole streets of lodging houses or parades and terraces interminable, in straight lines facing the sea, the roaring sea, and the severe gales, that make the frames of an invalid's bedroom casement rattle five days in the week at least, and shake his own frame in bed also ... An opportunity is now offered of establishing a real Montpelier on the South Coast of England, and a something better than a Montpelier in point of beauty, for the upper and wealthier classes of society.

Dr Granville followed this delightful fantasy with a warning of the danger of allowing the peace of Bournemouth to be spoilt by creating noises, bustle, confusion, vulgarity. He condemned elsewhere the 'interminable terraces, parades, and parabolas of houses of every sort and size and description, which mere brick-and-mortar speculators have run up'. He asked an embarrassingly blunt question: 'Is it then the intention of the three or four proprietors of the land at Bourne to act in the same manner?' If the proposed plan that he had seen was realised, then, he said with visionary fervour, 'the place will be in the category of those I have just painted; it will become one of twenty sea watering-places, just as tolerable and common, and will only be frequented as such, with slow progress and doubtful success.'

After this onslaught, which his audience of intending developers cannot have been happy to hear, he attacked Benjamin Ferrey's plan, made on behalf of Sir George Tapps-Gervis, for covering the face of the eastern slope above the Bourne with concentric circles of houses crowned with a Gothic church. His little sermon was taken to heart, for the erection of St Peter's church at the corner of Hinton Road (then Church Road) a few years later, was the final outcome. But while firmly recommending Bourne Mouth mainly as a resort for the sick and the devout, he did, however, believe it was suited also for people who, being otherwise well in health, like a retired rather than a bustling and noisy sea watering-place:

Bournemouth combines, to an eminent degree, the character of beautiful and sheltered rusticity with that of an open seaside residence ... To be near the sea and to be able to have recourse to its water or its breezes when necessary, yet not to be always and for ever saturated with either; to have it in one's power to turn to spots where its shingle-rustling or the loud roaring of its waves cannot disturb you — to be in fine, on the threshold between sea and land life, so as to take to each alternately as required, as a means of recovery from disease, or for the restoration of lost strength ... These are the advantages which, in my estimation, nature affords to an extent ... unequalled in any other place I am acquainted with on the South Coast of England.

Turning away finally from the attractions of Bourne Mouth as an invalid resort, Dr Granville gave a little advice as to how in his opinion it should be developed, much of which within the next few years was carried out. He recommended that the ramshackle wooden bridge across the Bourne should be replaced by a handsome stone one; that what he called the 'species of narrow flat prairie which divided the Bourne's two banks', should be transformed into a 'regular promenade garden all the way, with parterres and beds of flowers by the sides of the brook'.

Dr Granville's praise of Bourne Mouth in his book and his opinions of its value as a resort for 'tender invalids' set the marine village on the road to further growth and development. It was symbolised in 1843 by the arrival of a resident physician, Dr Mainwaring, who set up in practice in the belief that he would never lack for patients. And, noted the *Salisbury & Winchester Journal* (16 May 1842), 'there are likewise settled a grocer, a baker and a butcher, in addition to which there is a daily supply of fish, mutton, milk and vegetables from the neighbouring markets and villages.'

Perhaps somewhat offended by Dr Granville's criticisms, Benjamin Ferrey, architect to the Gervis estate, resigned a year or two later and was succeeded by the prestigious Decimus Burton, who, among many other things, had designed the triumphal arch at London's Hyde Park Corner, leading into the park. Having studied not just the Gervis estate, but the entire area of Bourne Mouth and its surroundings, Burton drew up a sequence of proposals for its development, quoted in Mate & Riddle's *Bournemouth, 1810-1910*. Those of them which were carried out greatly influenced the shape of Bournemouth.

He recommended that Mrs Tregonwell, owner of land on the valley's west side should be invited to co-operate with the trustees in a 'general plan for laying out this portion of the ground' and this she accepted. He strongly opposed any kind of architectural formality, in the belief that Bournemouth was distinguished by its 'rusticity', which if kept in being, would attract many appreciative visitors. So, he advised that care should be taken in thinning out the belts of pine trees, while walks and drives among them should be made. Significantly, he recommended that 'a wide Esplanade on the Cliff' should be constructed to extend from Boscombe chine as far as the county borough in the west, even beyond if possible'; and that 'ornamental pleasure grounds' should be laid out south of what is now the Square, from the beach to the Poole Road bridge.

But far from content simply to recommend, Burton took note of what was actually carried out, and reported accordingly to the Gervis Estate in May, 1849:

The fir plantation between the Westover Road and the sea, together with a portion of the sandy waste purchased of Lord Malmesbury, at the north of the valley, has been laid out as pleasure grounds by contract entered into with Mr Ramsey [a local nurseryman]; the brambles and rubbish have been cleared away, glades formed, paths made, a turf bank enclosure fence raised along the south-western boundary, and many thousands of ornamental shrubs planted. This spot has by this means been rendered a most agreeable and convenient promenade to visitors, and will be a means of attracting families of respectability to Bournemouth.

Respectability meant families of at least good social and financial standing, for only to these were the trustees of the Gervis estate willing to make their part of Bourne Mouth available. Among such visitors in the eighteen-forties were the Duke and Duchess of Montrose, the Duke of Argyll, the Marquis and Marchioness of Westminster, and the Lord and Lady Lytton. Thus, the little marine village had become the embodiment of the landowners' dreams, or, in a phrase, the 'resort of a select and fashionable assembly'! Their accommodation was catered for not only by the two hotels and the houses for rent in Richmond Terrace and Westover Villas, but by a cluster of new and attractive boarding houses — Heathfield Lodge, Windsor Cottages, Bourne Villa, Eagle's Nest, Essex Cottage, Rose Cottage, Sea View House, Morley House, Clarence Cottage and Willow Cottage, cottage in this context, meaning eight or nine bedrooms.

Better transport followed. The stage coach, *Emerald*, plying with foaming nags the rough tracks between Weymouth and Southampton, had hitherto skirted Bourne Mouth, but in 1840 it began carrying visitors in and away every morning, thus regularly linking the village with the wide world for the first time. It was a boon extended in 1847, when a branch of the South Western Railway's London/Southampton line via Wimborne and Wareham to Dorchester, was opened, bringing ever more of the sick — and the fit as well. Descending at Chrischurch Road or Poole stations, they had then only a short journey by coach to their little marine homesteads.

So, better transport encouraged more people to visit and to stay, and by 1851 the resident population reached just a few less than 700. Good quality houses and land upon which to build them were urgently needed. Opportunely, another big estate came on the market in 1851, through the death of Miss Bruce, the mysterious Scottish lady whose Branksome Estate extended along the Poole Road up to Talbot Woods and down as far as the Dorset coast. Mr Robert Kerley, of whom we shall hear more, bought some of this land at Westbourne, including parts west of Alum Chine, while Mr C.W. Packe, MP, purchased land to the west of Broad (now Branksome) Chine, where in due course he had the mansion named Branksome Tower built.

The sale of other parts of the Branksome Estate was well publicised. 'There has long been a demand for houses, as well as for residents as for visitors, but there has not been any adequate supply of sites suitable for building purposes until the present time,' announced an advertisement in the *Poole Herald* of May, 1852. 'The proprietors of the Branksome Estate, which comprises both sides of the Bourne Valley to the extent of more than two miles in length, are now prepared to offer to the public the most eligible sites for building ... Roads have been formed and various other important improvements have been made and are now in progress, for bringing into notice the capabilities of this lovely locality, which, for all purposes of health or enjoyment, is not to be surpassed in England.'

The newspaper gave the advertiser useful editorial support: 'The rising grounds on either side of the Bourne,' it declared, 'afford sites for building of unequalled beauty, and in the greatest variety; nor is this all, the roads, which are in course of making, amongst these hills, will bring into view all that diversity of scenery with which the country abounds. It may not be out of place to notice, incidentally, that the demand for labour is so large in the neighbourhood that none but the wilfully idle need lack employment.'

So, Bournemouth, as people referred to the little marine village by 1850, seems to have become a paradise for everyone — landowners, builders, developers, hoteliers, shopkeepers, physicians, parsons, the sick, the healthy and the active; for everyone, that is, except Mary Clapcott and William, her son, because the wide acres of the Dean Estate — apart from the rough heath land to the west regained from William Fryer — remained frozen in the grip of a mortgage. What her feelings about it were we can only imagine, although she had good but secret reason, to know that in the end she would triumph.

Meanwhile, despite this, for mother and son life was still dogged by anxiety. From all the property but the Littledown House estate, the produce and rents were consigned to William Fryer, together with the interest due on the mortgage. But in 1849, he had attained the age at which he felt the need to put his business affairs in order, so he asked Mary Clapcott, who was herself 77 years old, to arrange the repayment of the £15,000 he had lent to her through the mortgage, and this, of course, she could not do. Having no other alternative acceptable to her, she followed in her late husband's footsteps and turned elsewhere for the money, arranging for the mortgage to be taken over until 4 January 1856 by three local people on the fringe of country banking. They were Walter Long, Francis Locke and the Reverend John Paddon, a clergyman whose religious zeal was not dimmed by his money interests.

The new mortgage of the same lands and properties came into effect in October, 1849; but for one reason or the other life seems to have become even harder subsequently, for Mary and William. They had almost no ready money to pay their daily living expenses. At her wits' end Mary consulted a Mr Edward Hennings and his wife, Mary, who were known to lend money at the rate of five per cent. As security, Mary Clapcott deposited with them the title deeds to the Muckle-shell Estate, inherited from her father. The first loan, made in March 1850, amounted to the odd sum of £227 4s, for which she signed a promissory note agreeing to repay with interest in six months, which she did. The second loan, for £222 16s, followed four months later, while the first was still current. Subsequently, having repaid both these two loans, she was driven to borrow £150 for six months in March 1851 and £146 7s in January, 1852, this one being signed also by her son William. And with him, on 8 July 1854, she signed her last promissory note in shaky hand-writing. Three days later this unfortunate old lady died, aged 82, having been hounded for debts nearly all her life since marriage, mainly as a result of an error of judgement 50 years earlier by her father.

Her death and burial in Holdenhurst churchyard was for William a severe blow, because apart from the natural emotional tie between them, his mother was the only really close friend that he had ever had, with the exception of Jane Dean. His sense of isolation, of being a man apart, would therefore have been intensified, yet despite this and the impression that his awkward shyness gave those who came in contact with him, he was still a robust character, in no sense a man of straw. And now that everything depended upon him, he set about discovering how much his inheritance was worth when all debts had been paid — if this was found to be possible.

Apart from a few small legacies his mother had left the entire estate to him. As his lawyer declared it for probate, it amounted to 1,484 acres, including Littledown House and its contents, the land in and around Bournemouth, three farms and nine cottages. Assessed for succession duty — as it was then — it had a saleable value of £28,584 6s 2d producing an annual income of £1,425, most of which, of course, went to the three mortgagees of the estate, the Reverend John Paddon, Walter Long and Francis Locke. Succession duty, payable for a lineal descendant at the rate of one per cent, left William

Clapcott with a bill for about £286, to be paid by eight half-yearly instalments, the first, 12 months after his mother's will was proved, the seven other instalments every six months afterwards. However, the Inland Revenue at that time traditionally gave successors considerable latitude, so he was not hard-pressed from this quarter.

What about the outstanding mortgage on some 800 acres of the estate? If these needed to be sold to redeem the mortgage William would witness the fortune created by his grandfather and great-grandfather reduced to less than half of its value in 1854. Far from penury this would be, certainly, but still a disaster, yet there seemed to be no alternative.

But incredibly, Mary Clapcott many years earlier anticipated such a misfortune, although only when her lawyers began in leisurely fashion to examine her estate in detail was the full extent of her foresight revealed, foresight that by enabling the Dean Estates to be kept intact, also contributed to the attractive development of Bournemouth in the 19th century.

CHAPTER 6

Creeke's Plans

IT WAS A curiously unsophisticated man who inherited the Dean estates in 1854. The main interests of William Clapcott, shy, black-bearded, aged 42, were then the farm animals, horses and fox-hunting. So far, he had had no experience of business or estate management, having accepted all his adult life that this should rest on the shoulders of his dominating and capable mother. After the death of her husband, whose stewardship had been so ruinous, she had assumed full responsibility, an unspoken decision that William had never questioned. She had struggled with their constant burden of debt, had borrowed the money they needed for their daily needs while, ironically, owning and living in one of the region's finest houses. Up to her death, he had lived a life so sheltered, and consequently so lacking in the know-how that comes of business and social accomplishments that he had grown up strangely innocent of the ways of the world.

Suddenly, the weight of this great property inheritance, with its huge debt of £15,000, fell on his unready shoulders, an unwelcome burden. Then, a day or two after his mother died, Mr Thomas Rawlins (senior), the family solicitor, drove up to Littledown House in his pony and trap as the autumn leaves were falling to tell him how she had contrived that her death would end the burden. He revealed that in 1800, soon after her marriage, Mary Clapcott had secretly insured her life with the Rock Life Assurance Society for the relatively modest sum of £2,500, but in 1826, when her husband began to borrow heavily to pay his banking losses, she had taken out another life policy, this time for the substantial sum of £12,500 with the Equitable Life Assurance Society, which had already, it is interesting to note, been established for more than 60 years. And now that his mother was dead the insurance had become payable.

Having given the astounded William Clapcott this account of his mother's financial acumen, Mr Rawlings handed him a banker's order for £16,500 — over the years bonuses had increased the value of the policies by another £1,500. Even William's habitual reserve would have been dented by the sight of this cheque for such a large sum. For the first time in his life, the spectre of debt was banished. We can imagine that he was perhaps speechless, overcome by emotion at this revelation of his mother's thought and care for his life after her death.

But why had she kept the policies secret all these years? The most likely reason is that she wished her son to receive his inheritance intact, absolutely free of all debt, in the hope that he would, like the Deans of Holdenhurst, add to it in his lifetime and bequeath it to his own descendants. In advance of her time, she was markedly feminist, a believer in female dominance, and perhaps having regard to her husband's business failures she had good reason.

These windfall policies had transformed William's world. He was now a land magnate in truth. He could contemplate and enjoy the attractive surroundings of Littledown House and the Dean Estates knowing with delight that they belonged to him entirely. Or, at least, they would within a short time, after the completion of certain legal formalities upon which the mortgagees, the Reverend John Paddon and his friends insisted.

The mortgage which they had granted William's mother stipulated repayment on 4 January 1856, and, receiving interest at the top rate of five per cent, they firmly declined to accept repayment a day earlier. So, the documents reveal, it was agreed between William and Thomas Rawlins, that the £15,000 would be invested meantime in government bonds. These would be sold in due course and the proceeds be paid on 4 January 1856 to the reverend gentleman and his associates, with the interest on the bonds meantime paid to William, which from his point of view was a sensible arrangement.

He also received the £1,500 bonus from the insurance

policies, so despite all the bills with which he knew he would soon be faced, he felt he had a little money to spare to attire himself more like the prosperous country gentleman that his inheritance made possible. So, he embarked on a cautious spending spree. For the first time in his life he ordered entire outfits of new clothes: a dozen suits of the rough brown tweed he had so often wanted, several riding jackets, breeches, boots and hats from Webber's new shop in Commercial Road; shirts, ties, underclothing, socks and fine lawn handkerchiefs from Rogers' shop nearby. When these had been delivered, tried on and worn for the first time and the old threadbare clothes disposed of, he no doubt looked almost a different man, slightly less shy, less apart from other men. Perhaps, at this time, he began to wear the friendly, cheerful expression depicted in a portrait of him painted by an unknown artist a few years later.

Next, came the matter of his own name, for his grandfather, William Dean, had directed in his will that he must change his name to Dean by Royal Licence within a year of receiving his inheritance, or forfeit the vast property in favour of his cousin, Richard Dean. So, in late 1854, Thomas Rawlins applied to George Harrison, Esquire, Windsor Herald at the College of Arms, and in due course, after payment of the customary fee, on 25 July 1855 William's surnames became Clapcott Dean, which was his mother's preference, and in step with the then growing fashion for double-barrelled names.

These relatively minor expenses apart, he was faced with lawyers' bills, long-outstanding debts, Littledown House repairs, the cost of bigger stables and kennels, accommodation for more estate workers. Interest on the £15,000 due to the mortgagees and what remained of the £1,500 bonus, merely covered his living costs, so he needed more money soon. Fortunately, he knew where to turn for it, while he considered the sale of land. First, in November, 1854, he borrowed the fairly small sum of £200 from those ever-ready lenders, the Hennings, for two months. Next, on 11 January 1855, he turned to his aunt, Mrs Elizabeth Clapcott, of Evershot, Dorset, who lent him £1,000 at five per cent without security. On 4 January 1856, the Reverend Paddon and his associates received their £15,000, and the Dean Estate deeds were at last returned, entirely free of mortgage, after so many years. The income from

Pigshoot and Carew's farms and several cottages also came his way with the ending of the mortgage.

A little later, in September 1855, there is something of a mystery in William's life. Still residing in his new-found security at Littledown House, he rented at Holdenhurst from George Ferrey, Master of the Hospital of St Mary Magdalen at Christchurch, a secluded house with several acres of land adjoining Littledown. The annual rent was £10, payable half-yearly, 'on the Feast of the Annunciation of the Blessed Virgin Mary, and St. Michael the Archangel'.

For whom was this little house intended? Unlikely it is that he would have leased something of this style with several rooms for any of his staff at Littledown. For whom then, did he take possession of it? Certainly not for himself, for he was obliged to reside at Littledown. The most likely answer is that there was a woman in William's life and that the woman was his cousin, Jane Dean. Her sister, Elizabeth Cooper, had either already moved, or was about to move to Pembroke, in Wales. Alone, and still single herself, the prospect of living quietly as mistress of the man she would have liked to marry, in this secluded house, whose garden adjoined the Littledown estate, could well have meant happiness for her. There is no record of her ever having married, nor is it likely that he had since his mother's death met another woman whom he wished to house.

Equally unlikely is it that William, who clearly enjoyed the physical side of life, was prepared to live like an anchorite, alone in his isolated mansion, with no woman to share his table and his bed, to bring him the blessings of her feminine company. It is a fair assumption that cousinly love in this family had triumphed again and that William had leased the house near Littledown for Jane Dean, and the enjoyment and convenience of them both.

Soon after this, William exhibited his abysmal ignorance of Bournemouth property values, the one subject in which by now he should have been expert. On 14 February 1856, he concluded the sale to Mr Robert Kerley, a local farmer and landowner, of 137 acres of the Dean Westcliff estate (segment number 48 in the Enclosures Award of 1802 to William Dean) for the sum of £2,269 7s 4d, or about £16 an acre, far less than prices paid for nearby land for more than 40 years. Lewis

Tregonwell had paid £20 an acre in 1810, £40 in 1814 and £60 in 1822, while even in 1851 George Durrant had paid £86 an acre for 30 acres, near the Decoy Pond. Certainly, the land that William sold — the very same that his mother Mary Clapcott had persuaded the banker William Rolles Fryer to release from mortgage — bounded now by Alum Promenade, Alum Chine, Poole Road and the county boundary — was about a half mile from the village centre, but that hardly made it worth so little. It was a failure through ignorance on William's part that in time cost the Dean Estate dear.

Only four years later, Robert Kerley sold 45 acres of the land, no doubt at a handsome profit, to Mr C.A. King, for whom the architect Edward Buckton Lamb designed the house named Branksome Dene there. Years later, it is worth recalling, Lord Wimborne bought it, and in 1892 invited his brother-in-law Lord Randolph Churchill's family, to spend the summer there. The steep chine was the scene of an accident that in time could have been fateful for Great Britain. Young Winston Churchill, then a boy, leapt from the chine bank into the top branches of a pine tree, crashed to the ground almost 30 feet below and nearly lost his life.

Robert Kerley subsequently developed the estate by selling another big slice of land upon which the house Alumhurst was built in 1863, then still more land for the Herbert Home for convalescents and later, land for a number of smaller houses near the Poole Road. By one of the ironies of history Robert Kerley was the grandson of the Robert and Ann Kearley (as they spelt their name then) who were part owners of Littledown House in 1798, through inheritance from John Strong, an inheritance carrying a debt to William Dean. They had been obliged to sell out to him, so it could be said that in Robert Kerley's gain and William Clapcott Dean's loss there was some rough justice.

But in 1856 a chance to take part in local public life came William's way. How in character, was his reaction, we shall see. Bournemouth at this time, remained a marine village of great charm and beauty, with a population of seven or eight hundred, but it still lacked surfaced roads, paved sidewalks, a piped water supply, road lighting, a sewage system, a hospital, a school, a fire service or even any municipal organisation able to look after the community's material needs. Yet, as land-owners great and small sold plots for development, and the houses that builders erected found immediate buyers, the needs of the community at large became urgent.

Those residents who perceived that this condition of local anarchy could not go on for much longer, attended a meeting on 29 August 1854 and voted to seek parliamentary approval for a Bournemouth Improvement Bill, to enable representatives appointed from among local people to carry out the much needed improvements by means of money levied through rates.

The Bill, approved by Parliament in July 1856, provided for the appointment of a Board of 13 Commissioners with powers to carry out the impovements, and also to establish a market-place for the sale of useful commodities; to construct a jetty, pier or landing place, and by agreement to purchase or rent land desirable for the purpose of ornament, recreation, or improvement. The Lord of the Manor and a nominee chosen by him were to be permanent members, while the other eleven were to be elected subject to ownership of property with an annual value of £30 within the district assigned to the Commissioners, that is, 'within the circle of the radius of a mile, whereof the centre is the front door of the Belle Vue Hotel'. The eleven named commissioners were Samuel Bayly, William Clapcott Dean, Robert Kerley, George Ledgard, Charles William Packe, William Robson, Thomas Shettle, David Tuck, John Tregonwell, Samuel Thompson and William Esdaile Winter.

The Act authorised the Commissioners to levy a 'general improvement rate' not exceeding three shillings in the £ in any year on the annual value of the property assessed. Their first meeting was held on 30 July 1856, just seven members attending, William Clapcott Dean being among the absentees. According to the records, he failed subsequently to attend a single meeting; but even had he done so he would most likely have arrived in hunting attire, too shy to make a single statement or answer a question. Six months later, he was disqualified for non-attendance.

The reason for William's non-attendance might well have been a feeling that he did not belong to the tight little group of local businessmen and landowners who made up the Commissioners, some of whom appear to have won their appointments mainly to benefit themselves financially. When, for example, in 1858, the Commissioners arranged a loan of £5,000 to build a pier on the beach near the Bourne estuary, the funds were deposited in the Poole Town & County Bank, a small private bank owned partly by George Ledgard, chairman of the Commissioners, and Richard Ledgard, the Commissioners' non-elected treasurer.

But, undoubtedly owing to a stroke of totally unexpected misfortune soon afterwards, the bank failed and defaulted. Only speedy action by the National Provincial Bank in advancing enough cash for the pier project to be continued, warded off an explosion that would have shaken the infant Improvement Commission to its foundations. Strangely enough, George Ledgard did not feel that speedy resignation was appropriate under the circumstances, and continued in office for another four years until 1862, when he was disqualified for non-attendance.

At their first meeting, the Commissioners made the noteworthy appointment of Mr Christopher Crabbe Creeke as Surveyor and Inspector of Nuisances, by which latter it may be safely assumed they meant the local drainage system, or lack of it. Aged 36, Christopher Creeke had evidently been practising in London as an expert on roads and drains. He had invented Creeke's Patent Drain, a salutary device widely used in the London boroughs, and it was doubtless this know-how that led the Commissioners to engage him for long-suffering Bournemouth, where there was ample scope.

But Christopher Creeke, who had come to Bournemouth mainly for the sake of his health, was by no means a mere layer of sewers and paver of roads. Although there is no record of his having qualified as an architect, he had been the second president in 1848 of the Architectural Association when he was only 28; he was also a founder member of the Association of Architectural Draftsmen. But the main abilities of this dominating and very confident man were in the field of town planning; and in Bournemouth his prime responsibility was to be the planning of new roads in developing areas.

For his annual salary of £50, Creeke himself proposed his

Christopher Crabbe Creeke, seen in a portrait by W. J. Warren, was made Bournemouth's first official architect and surveyor in 1856, when he was 36. William Clapcott Dean engaged him to plan the West Cliff and Dean Park estates. (Photo: SHAUN GARNER)

duties to be: 'To advise, report on and prepare estimates for any work from time to time contemplated by the Commissioners relating to the profession of Surveyor, Architect and Civil Engineer; to provide all the requisite plans, specifications, and superintendence of works carried out in such manner that there should be no extra charge for drawings, specifications or superintendence. As Inspector of Nuisances to carry out the duties prescribed by the 'Nuisance Removal Act' and supervision of sanitary matters as laid down by the Acts, so that the Commissioners should not be at any extra expense or charged for supervision.'

Clearly, Christopher Creeke had an extraordinary appetite for work, or, more likely, he simply wished to be 'monarch of all he surveyed' in the creation of a new town, and in the nineteenth, unlike the twentieth century, this was a fairly new experience. Roads, drainage and sewage were Christopher

Creeke's first thoughts. 'A considerable part of Mr Creeke's early years under the Commissioners,' said an observer, 'was devoted to levelling the surface of the roads — lowering here, raising there — gravelling, channelling and curbing; all spare soil being thrown over the cliffs!'

Christopher Creeke's able and energetic approach to the task of improving Bournemouth's roads in 1857 came to William's notice and, greatly in need of professional advice, he made the wise decision to engage him as surveyor and special adviser to the Dean Estates. It was a timely move, for the 1,400 acres of farm land, pasture, heath and cliffs facing the sea, belts of pines and a few farm workers' cottages, had remained unchanged for centuries. But in the late 1850s, William Clapcott Dean realised that if he were to continue residing at Littledown as laid down in his grandfather's will, he must follow in the footsteps of the other land magnates, devise a building scheme and, offering building plots for sale or lease, reap the financial benefits that the growth of Bournemouth made possible.

Christopher Creeke no doubt explained to William what was essential for the future prosperity both of Bournemouth and the Dean Estates — good quality building, attractive uniformity of style, no over-crowding, the preservation of the natural beauty of the land through the careful placing of roads, the preservation of mature trees and the planting of new young ones.

But where and how, should William begin? The lands that he had inherited were composed of the beautiful West Cliff area (less the valuable segment in the west he had sold to Robert Kerley), the Dean Park, Eastwood, Northwood, Holdenhurst, Manor Farm, Littledown, Longbarrow and Queenswood estates. The West Cliff estate was bounded in the south by what is today part of the West Under Cliff Promenade, from Alum Chine almost to Bournemouth Pier, bounded in the west by Alum Chine and Grosvenor Road, to the north by

Overleaf:
Christopher Creeke's first plan for the layout of the Dean Park estate, here published for the first time, made widely extravagant use of the available land. It was subsequently redrawn on more economical lines.

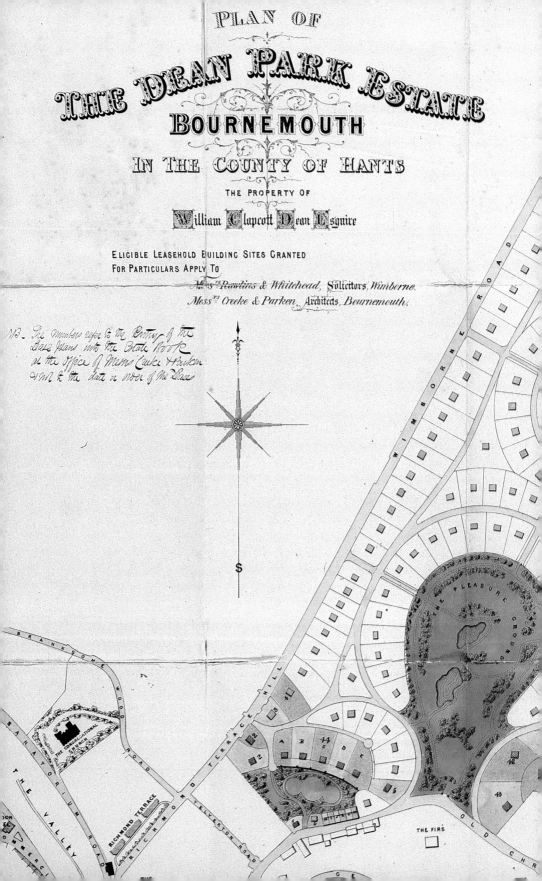

PLAN OF

THE DEAN PARK ESTATE

BOURNEMOUTH

IN THE COUNTY OF HANTS

THE PROPERTY OF

William Clapcott Dean Esquire

ELIGIBLE LEASEHOLD BUILDING SITES GRANTED
FOR PARTICULARS APPLY TO

~~Messrs Rawlins~~ *& Whitehead, Solicitors, Wimborne.*
Messrs Creeke & Parken, Architects, Bournemouth.

NB – The Numbers refer to the Entry of the Lease Plans into the Estate Book at the Office of Messrs Creeke & Parken and to the date or order of the Lease

S
WIMBORNE ROAD
BRANKSOME WOOD ROAD
SANATORIUM ROAD
THE VALLEY
THE CONGREGATIONAL CHURCH
RICHMOND TERRACE
RICHMOND ROAD
RICHMOND TERRACE HILL
YELVERTON ROAD
THE PLEASURE GROUND
THE FIRS
OLD CHR
A
B
C
D
E
44
4
3
2
2
5
42
43

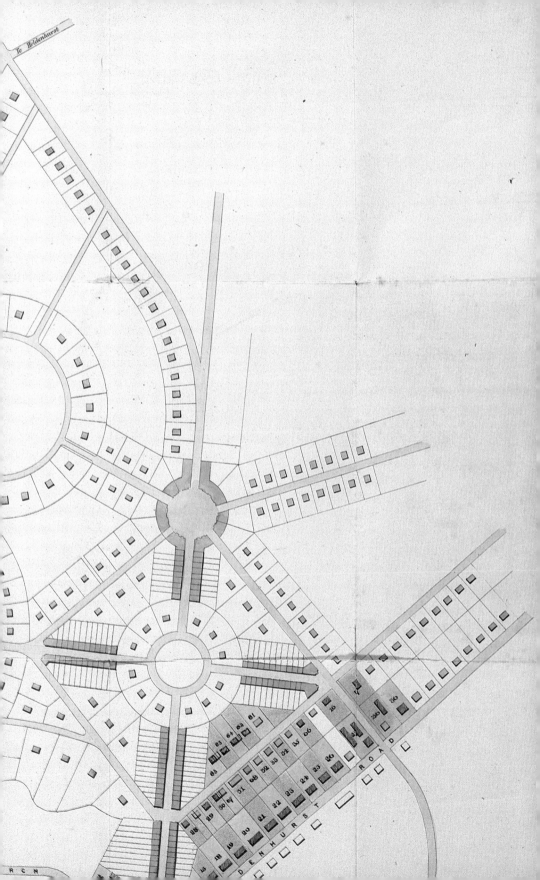

To Holdenhurst

DENHURST ROAD

Poole Road and to the east by West Hill Place and West Hill Road.

Separated from it by Commercial Road and The Square, lay the no less valuable Dean Park estate, extending north from, and including, an area enclosed by Old Christchurch Road, Albert Road, the east side of Richmond Hill leading to the east side of Wimborne Road; Charminster Road and Lowther Road to Hodenhurst Road, then back southwards to Old Christchurch Road and Albert Road. To the north-west of it lay the smaller Northwood estate, bounded by St. Luke's Road, Grafton Road to Iddlesleigh Road, Charminster Road and Wimborne Road; to the east but some distance away) is the Eastwood estate, bounded by Queen's Park South Drive, Richmond Park Road and the Holdenhurst Road. The Holdenhurst estate included the Longbarrow and Queenswood estates and Manor Farm, while the Littledown House estate extended from Castle Lane East, south-west to King's Park Drive. (Some road names of fairly recent origin which did not then exist are given to make identification easier.)

This, then, was the extent of the Dean Estates and one can imagine the unsophisticated William's utter perplexity as to how he should go about developing this huge acreage that he had inherited, in a place where land values, owing to natural beauty in a health-giving environment, were rising as fast as anywhere else in England. What, he wondered with some anxiety, should he instruct Mr Creeke to do? Arrange the sale of enough land for the best price he could get, so that he could live comfortably and quietly? Or, design some kind of building scheme and sell off plots to the many builders ready to bid for them? Finally, he did the most sensible thing, called in Christopher Creeke and instructed him to produce an overall plan upon which they could begin building development one way or the other.

And so began the creation of Bournemouth on the Dean Estates.

Creeke's first plan for the West Cliff estate development, illustrated his total dislike for straight roads; his liking for crescents, circular gardens, huge circuses of big detached villas, and tree-lined avenues that curved upon themselves with a grace and elegance which retired residents with time to spare found delightful, but strangers in a hurry found galling and frustrating.

A new road (now Durley Chine Road) running north from the coast beside Durley Chine up to and over Poole Road and on towards the present Wessex Way, was one of the main features of the plan actually carried out. Along what is now part of West Cliff Road the plan envisaged back-to-back residential crescents to crown a wide expanse of public gardens running north-west, divided by this new road and surrounded by large detached villas in the present Cresent Road and Chine Crescent.

Between the existing Durley Chine Road and Middle Chine, on the site of the present Cherry Tree Walk, Christopher Creeke planned another circus of large detached villas surrounded by more public gardens, linked by the road that now comprises the serpentine Overcliff Drive to, surprisingly, a broad and straight avenue running north-west for some 600 yards up to another huge residential circus, boardered on its outer circumference by more large detached villas, and containing within it a big church in an extensive graveyard.

The newly fashionable frolic of sea bathing and the delights of sailing, pictured in this water-colour of about 1840, brought genteel acclaim to the fashionable little marine village of Bourne Mouth.

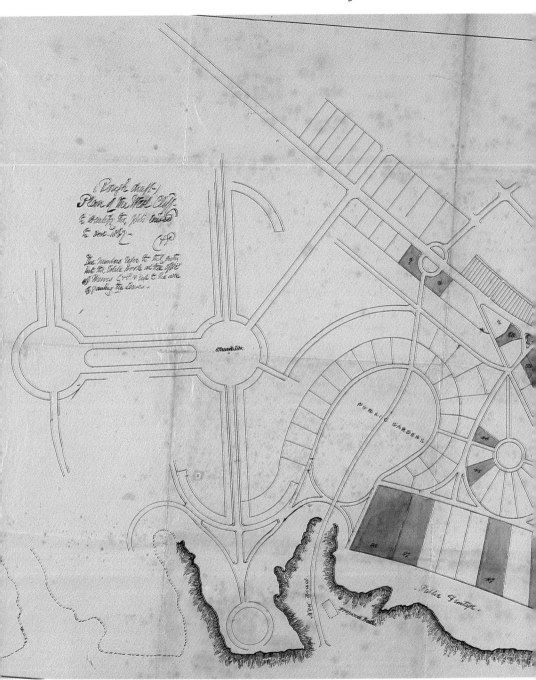

***Architect Creeke's grandiose plan for the West Cliff estate, though
lavish in its use of land, was accepted for the most part by William
Clapcott Dean, when he was a young, inexperienced man.***

From this circus, this main avenue also ran up to and over Poole Road in a north-westerly direction to today's Wessex Way, while from it ran four more straight avenues — north-west, west, north-east and south-east, linking 400 yards to the west with still another villa-encircled circus, with still more roads branching out.

Mr Creeke, it is evident, was, in terms of town planning an idealist. One of the two main features of this grandiose first plan was the sequence of over-sized residential circuses and crescents, linked together by broad tree-and-flower-lined single and double avenues. The other main feature was the lavish and extravagant use of limited and expensive land.

The same style governed the scheme he also submitted to William for the development of the Dean Park estate. Between Richmond Hill, Wimborne Road, Old Christchurch Road, Holdenhurst Road and what is now Lowther Road, he hopefully incorporated three splendid residential circuses, and a huge square surrounding a circus, each of them about the same size as the area contained by Cavendish Road including the cricket ground, or about six acres.

First, came Horseshoe Common, ringed by Dean Park Road, with six detached villas, divided by Richmond Gardens from another seven villas in Dean Park Crescent, all placed in about three acres of land each. Four of these villas faced across the road the green space which is today the Dean Park Cricket Ground (long may it stay with us!) which he named The Pleasure Gardens. These, he ringed by Cavendish Road and its circus of gracious detached villas on each side. Across the far side of what is now Lansdowne Road he conceived another similar grand residential circus surrounding more pleasure gardens.

In the easterly area towards Holdenhurst Road he devised a straight road north from the junction of Old Christchurch Road and Holdenhurst Road, running from north to south diagonally across a vast five hundred yard residential square, in whose centre he placed one more residential circus enclosing its inevitable eight-acre garden, bisected diagonally from east to west with another road that ran on to join up with Cavendish Road.

These then were in 1860 the stately plans for the development of the Dean Estates within the borders of Bournemouth, presented to William by the professional adviser upon whom he depended. We can imagine this unworldly land magnate seated at his desk in Littledown, staring in wonderment at the plans spread out before him, with their patterns of circles and crescents, endless gardens and wheel spokes of roads. With little or no knowledge of town planning, what was he to make of it? More than ever, he was perplexed, for he knew that he faced the responsibility of a decision that would affect both his own fortune and much of the shape of the future town of Bournemouth. On the one hand, it would be a mistake to tell a man of so independent a character as Christopher Creeke to try again, with another set of plans, for his answer could well be simply to break off the relationship and walk out. On the other hand, William clearly could not accept the plans in their present form. He was faced with a dilemma that the hardly knew how to solve.

CHAPTER 7

William Clapcott Dean

ALTHOUGH WILLIAM CLAPCOTT DEAN remained shy of people and public functions throughout his life he was by no means a nonentity. The possession of a great inheritance with its attendant problems inevitably added to his self-assurance and to his understanding of worldly concerns. After all, the ultimate responsibility for the development of the Dean Estates rested with him. There was no one else. The emperor's mantle had fallen upon his shoulders and he had no choice but to don it. He was, as we shall see, to wear it well, with authority and generosity.

But he was nevertheless at first a novice in the field of land development, reliant upon the advice of his surveyor, Christopher Creeke, who having produced detailed plans for housing in the Dean Estates, doubtless urged him to accept them as he had drawn them up. But studying them in the quiet of his study at Littledown, William evidently realised that while the West Cliff plans with some changes were suitable for what would obviously remain a mainly residential area, those for the Dean Park estate, where in contrast business premises were appearing, were wildly extravagant with land.

This estate covered some 600 acres, yet Christopher Creeke's plans showed sites for only 250 houses. What was said between the two in meetings about it was not recorded, nor to what extent Christopher Creeke defended the opulent style of planning of which he was so fond, but the outcome was a modified plan with greater density of housing between Lansdowne Road, Charminster Road and Holdenhurst Road, with similar though smaller changes between Westcliff Road and Poole Road.

William Clapcott Dean was quick to learn. The making of roads began, and he needed money for the contractors' bills. In February 1861, he mortgaged for the purpose 67 acres of pasture and arable land, including a farmhouse, a cottage and several barns at Muckleshell for £3,000 over ten years at four per cent with Mr James Rawlins, of Knowle Cottages, Beaminster, a relative of Thomas Rawlins. In contrast to the earlier mortgages with William Castleman arranged by his mother, he retained the rents and profits from these properties during the lifetime of the transaction.

At this time, he made an important decision regarding the Dean Estates. Probably on the advice of Christopher Creeke, he decided that no more land should be sold freehold; instead it would be sold on 99-year-leases. He was learning to safeguard his inheritance.

There was, however, an exception to this rule — a four-acre plot where Westcliff Gardens is now to be found which he had agreed to sell in 1860 to Thomas Rawlins. In 1861, Rawlins built a large bungalow-type house with a big square tower overlooking the coast and the sea, named West Cliff Cottage. But after his death in 1881, his executors demolished and replaced it with a block of inappropriate terrace houses in the centre of the property, surrounded by a rectangle of detached villas, and these still stand today.

At first Christopher Creeke demonstrated a preference for uniformity of design. One of the earliest parts of the West Cliff estate to be developed was an area surrounded today by West Hill Road, Poole Hill and Purbeck Road, including West Hill Place and Alma Place. Several builders, including Joseph Cutler, John Hibidage (both local Commissioners), Josiah Penney and William White, leased plots there to build small houses with shop fronts for artisans. But before completion of the contracts Christopher Creeke obliged them all to sign a covenant binding them among themselves to uniformity of design and elevation. It was a praiseworthy, but vain and short-lived attempt to keep architectural squalor out of Bournemouth.

The pace of building gained momentum, and from the 1860s onwards the little marine village, with its ramshackle pier, its rustic bridge spanning the Bourne stream and its villas

A paddle steamer coasting between Christchurch and Swanage embarks holidaymakers from the wooden pier built in 1861 at Bourne Mouth, as the little village was then called. Designed by James Rennie to be 1,000 feet long, it was too fragile and in January 1867 was damaged in a storm that swept away 300 feet and the T-ending. It was shortened to 600 feet.

of curious and incongruous design peeping through the belts of dark pines by the sea, began by degrees to be supplanted by the flourishing new seaside town. By 1862, 15 building plots on 99-year-leases had been sold in Chine Crescent Road, Durley Road, Chine Road and elsewhere in the Westcliff estate through the estate office conducted by Christopher Creeke and his architect partner, Charles Gifford. Bournemouth was becoming urbanised. By the end of 1864, in place of darkness at night William became used to twinkling lights in the distance below Littledown House.

Once having accustomed himself to the changing landscape, the purple, heather-covered heath giving way to roads and houses, he welcomed them, though not without regrets for the ancient vista over which he had ridden and hunted since boyhood that had gone forever. The first building plot on the Dean Park estate was sold in 1863, with a 99-year-lease on Richmond Hill, to Mr Charles Rose, a descendant of the Sir

George Rose who was old William Dean's principal trustee years earlier. He named the villa he built there Heatherbank, and he paid an annual ground rent of £10 for it. Later that year he leased another building plot on Richmond Hill, had a villa named Seymour Lodge built and let it to Mr Charles England.

Under Christopher Creeke's direction, Christchurch Road, Old Christchurch Road, Richmond Hill, Wimborne Road, Holdenhurst Road, Oxford Road, Lansdowne Road and other roads were in turn surfaced, curbed and equipped with drains. In 1863, the Bournemouth Gas and Water Company had begun to install lighting in these principal roads. Piped water followed, derived from springs of pure water that arose on moors behind the village and from a deep well nearby. Such public utilities were a further stimulus to development, and by the end of 1864 Charles Gifford had sold another nine plots in the Dean Park estate, 11 more in 1865, six of them in Holdenhurst Road, two in Richmond Gardens and three in Lansdowne Crescent. After a pause in 1866, 17 found buyers in 1867, chiefly in Old Christchurch Road and Oxford Road, but from 1868 to 1870 the pace slowed. It quickened again in 1871 with eight houses built variously in Dean Park Road, Lansdowne Road and Wimborne Road, 19 more in 1872 in Oxford Road and Dean Park Road, then 20 in 1873, three of the roads in the Westcliff estate — Chine Road, Chine Crescent Road and Durley Road — taking the lion's share.

Henry Laidlaw, a local businessman who in 1881 was to establish a much-needed and popular horse-drawn bus service between Westover and Boscombe, bought a plot in 1871 near Granville Crescent with a ground rent of £12 to build a substantial house with stables and spacious gardens. Next door, a few months later, the builder Joseph Cutler built a smaller house with a ground rent then of five guineas. By 1875 detached villas stood on both sides of most of the entirely residential Old Christchurch Road, but Lansdowne Crescent boasted a bevy of small shops patronised by local residents.

Building began in Lansdowne Road, a main artery of the Dean Park estate, in 1871, the first plot there going to Miss Hannah Santy, upon which she built her house, Hamilton Rise. The British School, run by local volunteer teachers, was opened at number 22 Lansdowne Road, on the corner of the still undeveloped Madeira Road, in 1875, the year that the Baptist Chapel also opened its doors. Thereafter, William Clapcott Dean was content to see plots sold and villas built in regular succession on both sides of Lansdowne Road, but it was not to be fully completed for more than 10 years. Plots for houses in the shorter Oxford Road, where building began in 1867, were sold more quickly. It was about complete by 1874, the year that houses first appeared in the estate's Heath Poult (later St Paul's) Road and Littledown Road, where a plot was acquired for that busy enterprise the Steam Laundry Company.

Road construction in the two estates meant big and continuous financial outlay, with the return on the investment at first relatively small, and dependent upon the rate at which building plots were sold, but William Clapcott Dean went about it with vision, a sense of scale and the knowledge that future generations rather than he himself would be the main beneficiaries. He had to find more working capital for the undertaking and on 19 April 1872 he mortgaged with a Mr William Udal, of Park Mount, Edgbaston, a farm at Holdenhurst and ground rents from 70 of the already leased plots, mainly in Holdenhurst Road and Richmond Hill, for the substantial sum of £9,000 at four-and-a-half per cent interest from 19 April to 19 October 1872, subsequently extended at yearly intervals, and finally repaid with the properties reconveyed to him in February 1880. To do this he unavoidably reduced his own income.

But William Clapcott Dean was not only interested in safeguarding the family fortune. He had a very real sense of responsibility towards the new town spreading below Littledown House. The Improvement Commissioners discovered that he took a paternal interest in up-and-coming Bournemouth and was willing to help provide for its needs.

One pressing need was for a cemetery. The many sick and old people who, often without much hope had come to Bournemouth in search of recovery, made death so constant a visitor that St Peter's burial-ground, like those of the parish churches of Holdenhurst, Moordown, Pokesdown, Throop and the Christchurch cemetery, was nearly full. The locally

Children play by the gardens of terraced houses built in 1864 by Joseph Cutler to designs by architect Charles Gifford in Holdenhurst Road, on the Dean Park estate.

appointed Burial Board, hunting for an available piece of land big enough for future needs, requested William Clapcott Dean, as one who they knew had the interests of the community at heart, to help.

Consulting with Christopher Creeke, William offered 22 acres of the Northwood estate at Rush Corner, the junction of Charminster and Wimborne Roads (it was Enclosure Award No 143 to William Dean), at a nominal price. Accepting the offer with thanks, the Chairman of the Board declared that Mr Clapcott Dean 'had acted very handsomely'.

The land was duly conveyed, and Christopher Creeke designed the cemetery chapel. This having been built in 1877, the invitation to lay a memorial stone was made, but not to William Clapcott Dean, the obvious choice, but — so incorrigibly class-conscious was the little town then — to Sir George Meyrick. That ubiquitous local builder and Burial Board member, Joseph Cutler, then proposed that the avenue from the main cemetery gates to the chapel should be beautified with macabre golden holly and (that most repellent of trees) the monkey puzzle. Obligingly, the Board agreed and awarded him the contract to purchase and plant the trees. The cemetery came into use in April 1878, and doubtless those people nearing their end in Bournemouth slept more soundly.

Provision of land for this mundane purpose was only the

beginning of William's generosity. The extent to which he contributed to Bournemouth's development by outright gifts and leases of land at nominal rents never became public knowledge. He was, in fact, one of the town's true but unrecognised fathers, a compassionate man with deep sympathy for the poor, whose numbers in the 1870s included those men he would have been closest to — farm labourers suffering from the agricultural depression that countrywide forced 100,000 of them from the land as the acreage under wheat declined.

Compassion and the will to help grew from sympathy. His first concern was for the impoverished sick. In 1874, he made an outright gift of a large plot of land near St Peter's church as a site for the Firs Home. A sanatorium for poor and incurable tuberculosis sufferers, it was founded by the Reverend S. W. Waddelow and supported entirely by voluntary grants and subscriptions.

He responded generously again to a request for charity in 1877, when the trustees of the Hahnemann Convalescent Home & Homeopathic Dispensary, a trust founded in Germany, asked for his help with land for the establishment of a convalescent and nursing home in Bournemouth. It was designed for sufferers with a fair hope of recovery from tuberculosis, that scourage of the nineteenth century. William obliged with a 999-years-lease of a site on the West Cliff at a nominal ground rent of £1 1s a year. The building was completed in 12 months and opened on 3 June 1879. The need for its original purpose having long since gone, it is now, as part of the East Dorset Health Authority, run as a convalescent facility.

Although himself a member of the Church of England, William was not deaf to the needs of other denominations, and in 1876 he made available, for a low rent, a long-lease site for the Baptist Church in Lansdowne Road, which still stands today. And also in that year, when St Peter's Church wished to establish a school, he provided a suitable site in St Paul's Road, again with a 99-year-lease at a low rent. The school was named St Paul's School.

The needs of the churches and the sick apart, he supported the education of working people and their children at a time when State-aided schools were in their infancy, and teaching was still mainly the work of Church Schools, excepting of course the Public Schools and Grammar Schools. In June 1877, he made an outright gift of a valuable piece of land bounded by West Hill Road and West Cliff Road, on the West Cliff estate, for a Church of England School and master's house, under the wing of St Michael's and All Angels' Church nearby. Called St Michael's School, its declared purpose was the teaching of 'children and adults, or children only, of the labouring, manufacturing and other poorer classes in the said district of St Michael...' The deed of gift stated that the school and house were to cost no less than £1,000; that William Clapcott Dean would build a three-foot-high brick wall around the site and that he would be responsible for the laying and maintenance of drains and roads to it. The school was to be governed by the vicar, the Reverend Edward Wanklyn and the members of a church committee, who, it is interesting to note, had sole rights to select the books to be used for teaching the children.

William believed it was proper that the vicar of the newly-built church, which had been consecrated in 1876, should be

This legal document embodied William Clapcott Dean's gift in 1871 of a site for St. Michael's School and master's house.

Dated 9th June 1[...]

West Cliff Estate

Bournemouth.

Grant

— of —

A piece of land and premises on the West Cliff Bournemouth for the site of a School and Masters House &c.

able to reside as near as possible to church and school, and that land should be made available for the purpose. He himself therefore made another outright gift of a plot of land adjoining the school, upon which the vicarage was built. It is today part of the school.

Apart from these and other gifts of land for religious and educational purposes, he gave generously for sporting activities. He used to attend matches between the Reverend Wanklyn's Pupils' eleven against visiting teams, played on the meadows of what became the Upper Pleasure Gardens (now Pine Walk), and later, on the pitch at Springbourne, home of the then newly-formed Bournemouth Cricket Club. This ground was found to be inadequate by 1869, so either the Club approached him, or more likely he offered the seven acres of the circular plateau of ground with its fine level surface near Horseshoe Common, ringed by what became Cavendish Road. Negotiations were concluded in 1869 for the lease of the land at a nominal price, and in 1870 the turfing, building of a pavilion, the making of tennis-courts, croquet ground and a bowling-green began.

The first ever cricket match on what became known as the Dean Park Cricket Ground was played on 30 June 1871, between the Bournemouth Cricket Club and the officers of the Royal Artillery then stationed at Christchurch, since which the crack of ball against bat has never ceased in summer to echo. Hants Cricket Club play county matches there. Remarkable and attractive is, of course, the splendid situation in the town centre of this cricket ground, a boon that all, from the cricketing public to the Bournemouth municipality, must wish to last for all time.

But the popularity of sport in Bournemouth was dwarfed in the 1870s by the extraordinary surge in church-going there, where many people felt that a second church of the Church of England more evangelical in character than St Peter's was needed. The Church of the Holy Trinity was therefore built and consecrated in 1878 upon a site in Madeira Vale (now Stafford Road) given by Robert Kerley. When the need for a vicarage nearby arose William Clapcott Dean came forward with the gift of a spacious site. He might have been content thereby to take a little of the limelight from the man who persuaded him to part with a big slice of land for a song 20 years ago. Holy Trinity, like all too many churches in Bournemouth, a monument to overblown architectural ugliness, was deemed superfluous in 1973, deconsecrated and converted to a banqueting hall, until it was burned down in 1979, except for the tower, and this, three years later, was sensibly demolished.

Churches mushroomed in Bournemouth throughout the 1870s and eighties, for leaders of the many religious denominations thought it essential to provide facilities. By 1880 when the population was about 12,000, no less than 18 of them, ranging from orthodox Anglican to Roman Catholic, Primitive Methodist, Baptist, Presbyterian and Quaker called the faithfull to worship.

What impression did this abundance of spiritual guidance make upon articulate observers? We cannot unfortunately, include William Clapcott Dean in this category, but there was one whose comments are well worth reading. 'Bournemouth is ... a very pretty place; it is also a very strange place,' maintained the Hon. Grantley Berkeley in his autobiography, *Life And Recollections*. '...Week-days as well as Sunday, the apparently religious flock to their places of meeting ... From the way the churches were thronged, and the frequency of Divine service, I had thought at first that Bournemouth must rank high in sanctity and decorum, but on inspecting the visitors' list kept at the Library, I saw therein that no less than 27 fresh clergymen had arrived in one week. What then means this advent of religious men? Surely there must be some reason for their flocking here? Either the place has been very wicked, or it must become good.'

Wicked, a diminutive Monte Carlo, Bournemouth plainly never was, nor was it in the moral sense ever particularly good, although with their almost feverish church-going the affluent inhabitants exhibited a fervent desire to be accounted so in the eyes of the Almighty. Observers who saw Bournemouth then, aver that it was quiet and reserved, or sedate, prim and boring, according to their social preferences. Would the social milieu have encouraged William Clapcott Dean, to whom the epithet *good* in some ways could rightly be applied, to overcome his shyness, his awkwardness, and become one with it? Or was it of the kind that would have driven him away.

106

A small child sets off for a donkey ride in The Square in 1875, where the so-called Scotch church on the corner of Richmond Hill and Old Christchurch Road cast a bleak aura.

Contemporary observers of the social scene say little of the Bournemouth of those years that rings with enchantment. Philip Brannon (*Historical & Picturesque Guide to Bournemouth*, published in 1881) praised its quiet and seclusion, which, he fervently hoped, would be preserved for ever, a point of view firmly on the side of dreariness. Charles W. Wood, co-editor of the magazine *The Argosy*, labelled Bournemouth a melancholy place, while the then influential *Blackwood's Magazine*, reported that 'dances and light concerts are discouraged; and dissipation is said to take the shape of bazaars and social meetings for charitable objects'.

For a more exact picture, written in a vivid and amusing style we must refer again to Grantley Berkeley, who in 1860 lamented that at Bournemouth, 'man has no amusement of any kind; and what is stranger still, when man and woman meet ... there is no association, no promenade as at other places, where the people walk; and not an opportunity sought in which to exchange an idea.' Bournemouth, he declared, seemed to be 'made for social enjoyment and to awaken the heart to genial sympathy, yet the visitors apparently shrink within themselves, remaining in their lodgings or hotels...'

Finding the social scene dull and puritanical, he noted that the ladies 'bob about from dell to dell as if they thought every bush concealed a serpent and a tempting apple, and that they were never safe unless at church'. Grantley Berkeley planned to write a satirical play entitled *A Trip to Bournemouth*, part of the pointed prologue of which, aimed at the local young ladies, concluded:

> Enjoy your bath, your walk, your croquet game,
> And archery practise without fear or shame;
> Have your flirtations in a harmless way,
> Whether at concert, promenade or play,
> Pic-nic, or yacht excursions in the Bay,
> And cease to go to church three times a day.
> Remember, you need heed no harsh complaints,
> Those who are ANGELS never need be SAINTS.

If a seasoned socialite like Grantley Berkeley found Bournemouth life mindless and dim, what chance had a shy and eccentric outsider like William Clapcott Dean to make hay? He could only turn away from the spectral scene and cultivate his garden, so to speak, which with diligence he continued to do. So far as his personal life went, he seems to have been perfectly happy with the country pursuits that he had always enjoyed — to ride, hunt and shoot in the vicinity of Littledown House, where he was well served by his gamekeeper, Henry Plowman, his groom, William Vatter, his gardener, Charles Tanner, his foreman John King and his cook, Rebecca Best, both alone and accompanied by his sporting associates. Among the latter, were one or two unwise enough to take on a bet with William, who had a partiality for donkeys; he used sometimes to ride around the Littledown estate in a small cart drawn by two of them. In response to teasing by his friends he challenged them to a race up the steep ascent to Littledown, he in his donkey-cart and they in horse-drawn vehicles. He won, knowing through experience that his donkeys trotted faster up a steep hill than horses.

In his own acres, William Clapcott Dean was a robust and jovial eccentric, although to the burgeoning town of Bournemouth, he presented in his brown homburg and rough tweed suits the appearance of a sober and business-like Victorian gentleman. By now, he had developed very definite beliefs as to what was and what was not beneficial to the town. He paid, for example, the full cost of all the roads that Christopher Creeke had had laid on his behalf in the Dean Estate, and also half the cost of those laid there by the Improvement Commissioners, yet he strongly opposed schemes he considered needless, or mere embroidery, including the controversial project for an Undercliff Drive from Alum Chine eastwards to Boscombe.

For many years strong opinions for and against the project had been aired. Christopher Creeke had supported the Improvement Commissioners in their desire for it, pleading the benefits and attractions it would confer on the town. A scheme drawn up by Sir Joseph Bazalgette, engineer of the Thames Embankment, was opposed at a stormy meeting in 1878 by Mr John Tregonwell, who moved a resolution that it was 'an unnecessary and wasteful addition to the debts and liabilities which have already been contracted by the Commissioners at the expense of the ratepayers and to the detriment of house property in this place'. His resolution was carried and the plan dropped.

But only for two or three years. In 1882, Mr Eugenius Birch, a civil engineer who had designed the recently-built pier, presented a scheme for an Undercliff Drive to be constructed and financed through private enterprise, entirely

Holidaymakers parade in top hats and morning coats on Bournemouth east beach in 1875, obedient to local decorum. Wheeled bathing machines give cover to venturesome swimmers.

without cost to the ratepayers. It included on the landward side a 'bathing establishment', a museum, an aquarium and buildings devoted to the arts, sciences, health and gymnastic exercises, for all of which visitors would be charged to enter. The profits would go to the promoters to redeem the mortgages they had negotiated to pay their construction costs, estimated at a minimum of £70,000.

Surprisingly, the Improvement Commissioners viewed this scheme favourably, and backed it. But first, they needed the agreement and co-operation of William Clapcott Dean, who owned both the foreshore and the land behind. In December 1883, he received a letter from the Commissioners requesting 'permission to construct a public foot and carriage-way along the sea front of the West Cliff communicating with the public roads at St Michael's and Durley Chine Roads'. They also asked his permission to construct a foot and carriage-way from Durley Chine to the beach through Durley Chine — a proposal that, if carried out, would have ruined the Chine's natural beauty. William Clapcott Dean noted as well that the Commissioners made no request to lease or buy the land involved, but simply requested in effect that it should be handed over to them more or less to do with as they wished.

A measure of his indignation at the request was his absolute disregard of it. Patiently, knowing their man by now, the worthy Commissioners waited. A year, then two years went by, and still no answer. In desperation, they by-passed him and wrote appealing to his surveyor, Christopher Creeke. Perhaps hardened still more by this attempt to enlist his own man on their side, William made no reply to this letter either.

Finally, in 1887, in answer to still another letter, addressed to him, he replied, stating flatly that he did not require the Undercliff road to be made, and therefore could not enter into any agreement with the Commissioners relating to it. He added that he could not hand over any land on the cliff front of the West Cliff; also, that the use of his land at the East end must stand over until it was decided what form of development that portion of the estate should take. So far as he was concerned, that was that. On this issue, his known argument was that any expenditure on the West Cliff frontage should go to reinforcing the crumbling cliff face, rather than upon a vulnerable undercliff road.

110

In that same year of 1887, he made another outright gift of land of lasting value to the community. Several local gentlemen had together formed a trust to found a new hospital for the treatment of non-infectious diseases and accidents in Bournemouth. They were, for the record, Frederick Bright, Justyn George Douglas, M.D., George Robert Elwes (Captain, the 14th Hussars), William Fisher, Thomas James Hankinson, Henry Newlyn, Charles Jones Nixon, William Vicary Snow, M.D., Richard Stephens and John Thomson Roberts, M.D. These gentlemen, the trustees, decided to name the hospital the Royal Victoria Hospital, to commemorate the golden jubilee on 20 June 1877 of Queen Victoria's reign, and to raise the money to build it by public subscription. It was to replace the Bournemouth Public Dispensary first set up in 1859 at 2, Granville Cottages, later, in 1869, transferred to a larger site purchased from Robert Kerley near Holy Trinity church, which in the ever-growing town had again become too small.

So, early in 1887, while local women strove to raise money for the building by means of charity functions, the trustees grappled with the problem of finding a suitable site for as little expenditure as possible. Having had no success, so much had land values risen in Bournemouth, they approached William Clapcott Dean. It was wholly in character that he at once

This document embodied William Clapcott Dean's gift in 1887 of land for the Royal Victoria Hospital in Poole Road.

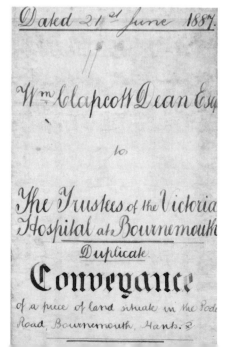

agreed to help. Having studied the site question, he offered the trustees the 22 acres of land where the hospital stands today, as an outright gift, demonstrating again his unequalled generosity towards the town. Valued then at £900, the land was gratefully accepted and a deed of gift drafted.

'Now this Indenture witnesseth,' stated the deed, dated 20 June 1887, 'that ... the said William Clapcott Dean doth hereby freely and voluntarily and without any valuable consideration convey unto the Trustees all that piece of land ... delineated and set out in the plan drawn in the margin ... And the Trustees hereby covenant with the said William Clapcott Dean that they ... will at all times hereafter use any Buildings to be erected on the said land as a General Hospital and Dispensary not for infectious diseases...'

Somehow, the local women's committees managed to raise the substantial sum of £8,300 needed to build the hospital, in excess of the £4,500 made over to the trustees from the Dispensary funds. And upon the day of Queen Victoria's Jubilee the foundation stone was laid on the site — not however, by the donor, William Clapcott Dean, or by one of the trustees whose brainchild the plan for the hospital was, but by E. W. Rebbeck, local estate agent and chairman of the Improvement Commissioners.

When building was about to start the importance of his gift was dramatically underlined. William Clapcott Dean, this shy gentle man who had done so much for Bournemouth with so little public recognition, died at the age of 75 in 1877 at Littledown House, and suddenly the hospital project was set at nought. Because his death occurred within 12 months of his gift, it became void under what was known as the Mortmain Act.

CHAPTER 8

The Cooper Inheritance

WILLIAM CLAPCOTT DEAN'S will held many surprises. He had left unusual legacies in favour not only of his trustees and his servants, but also of his horses and hounds. His personal estate amounted to £22,000 (worth about £770,000 in 1986) in cash at the bank and government securities, so he was able to be generous. In addition to this personal estate, he was handing down his life interest in the West Cliff and Dean Park estates in Bournemouth, as well as Carew's and Pigshoot Farms at Throop, and the splendid Littledown House estate, with its horses, hounds, farm animals, cottages and buildings. Excited speculation as to who would inherit this fortune there had been for some time. He had no children, no brothers and no sisters.

James Edward Cooper, his second cousin, aged 47, was a master builder in the city of York. He was a direct descendant of Richard Dean, brother of John Dean, the grandfather of Mary Dean, wife of William Clapcott, who had died in 1833. James Cooper's parents, Elizabeth Dean and Joseph Cooper, had in 1850 moved to Pembroke, where Joseph Cooper carried on business as an estate agent until his death a few years later.

They had three sons, all born in Holdenhurst, Joseph, the eldest, then Richard, and James, the youngest, who was apprenticed to a joiner and cabinet maker in Pembroke, George Barrett. But James was no ordinary carpenter. Completing his apprenticeship, he worked in Pembroke until his mother's death, after which, moving north to York, he prospered among the hard-headed Yorkshiremen as a master builder and occasionally as a practical architect, reputedly designing among other buildings the Belle Vue Gardens at Manchester.

On 5 December 1887 he received a letter from a Mr Henry Chislett. Surprisingly giving his address as Littledown House, Chislett reported the death of William Clapcott Dean who, so far as can be ascertained, James Edward Cooper had not seen for some years. Dr Stevens, his cousin's personal physician, and he himself, estate steward, were Mr Clapcott Dean's executors. 'I write asking you to attend the funeral on Saturday, because you are interested under the will. I cannot well in this letter tell you to what extent but I shall be prepared to do so on Saturday next,' he said, disdaining to disclose anything of the extent of the inheritance that was to come James Cooper's way — an ambiguity to which he added by stating that his brothers, Joseph and Richard, and their cousin, Dean Cooper, were also interested parties. It was James Cooper's first contact with the executors, that was to end in a High Court lawsuit.

The many beneficiaries under the will, masking high hopes behind grave faces, assembled at Littledown House after William Clapcott Dean's funeral and burial in the family vault in Holdenhurst churchyard in mid-December 1887, to hear Walter Rawlins, then the family solicitor, read the will, for it was he who disclosed the details, in his slow soft voice. Listening patiently among the motley assembly of interested men and women in their stiff black garments, James Edward Cooper finally comprehended through the web of legal terminology, that both as regards his dead cousin's personal fortune and the life interest in land and property, he himself was the main beneficiary.

It could well have taken his breath away, this change of status from that of prosperous artisan to land magnate, a wholly unexpected turn of the wheel of fortune. While he might have expected to inherit something from William Clapcott Dean, as the youngest of the three brothers he could not have anticipated this great windfall, custom then dictating that the bulk of an inheritance should pass to the eldest in line, with small legacies to the younger ones.

This was the will's main provision, but there were numerous others, one in particular affecting James Edward Cooper's inheritance. William Clapcott Dean had willed that he was to reside at Littledown House; but also that 'my trustees shall enter into possession of and the receipt of the rents of the said

Bournemouth inhabitants depended entirely upon horse transport in the 1880s and this bus picked up passengers by the Pier Hotel, while the horse drank at the trough. William Clapcott Dean drove down to the town from Littledown House in one of his carriages.

premises' for the term of a year and 'during the said period have the sole control over and manage such premises with all the powers of an absolute owner'.

From the rents and income arising out of the estates during this year the trustees had to pay 'as they thought fit' for any repairs and outgoings, and to keep any surplus for James Edward Cooper, but only 'as they thought fit' — in effect an invitation, he must have thought, to keep it for themselves. And so that the trustees need not pay him any money before their year in possession ended, they might, again 'if they thought fit', allow him to reside at Littledown.

One can imagine his feelings at this extraordinary clause giving the trustees so much power — hear him tell himself — 'I have inherited this place on condition that I reside here, yes, but I am told that I may not do so for the next 12 months unless the trustees graciously permit me to do so. Meanwhile, they have the powers of an absolute owner over the estate and may do with it whatever they wish except cut down trees and hold an auction on the premises' — for these were the sole prohibitions affecting them. 'I declare', the will stated, 'that my trustees shall not ... be entitled or have power to cut any timber ... except for repairs of farm buildings or otherwise to be consumed on the said premises, nor shall they or any other person whatever have power to hold any auction sale whatever on the said premises during the said term ... and my Will is that no trees shall at any time hereafter be cut under any circumstances in the Fir plantation forming part of my Freehold Estate adjoining Bournemouth Cemetery..'

Having no children upon whom to lavish love and money, William Clapcott Dean had turned to nature and animals. He loved his trees, but even more he loved his horses and his dogs. To them, had it been possible, he might well have left a fortune, but he did the next best thing. With what must have been amazement, James Edward Cooper heard the lawyer continue: 'I give to my trustees my eight horses and ponies (excluding cart horses) at Littledown and also my hounds in kennels there and I charge my said Freehold Estates ... in priority to all other charges created by this my Will with the payment to my Trustees for the term of 50 years commencing from my death (if any of the said horses and hounds shall so long live) of an annual sum of £750 payable quarterly ... and I declare that my Trustees shall apply the said annual sum ... in the maintenance of the said horses and hounds for the time being living, and in maintaining the stables and kennels and buildings now inhabited by the said animals in such condition of repair as my Trustees shall deem fit, but this condition shall not imply any obligation on my Trustees to leave the said stables and kennels in a state of repair at the determination of the said term..'

Thus to make the two trustees, Dr Stevens and Mr Chislett, the main beneficiaries next to himself, without any real obligations apart from payment of legacies was bad enough, but evidently it was the next clause that really exasperated James Cooper: 'I declare that my Trustees shall not be bound to render any account of the application or expenditure of the said sum of £750 and any part thereof remaining unapplied shall be dealt with by them at their sole discretion..'

Did this mean the Trustees were left the considerable sum of £750 a year (about £26,000 in 1986) to spend more or less as they wished for as long as any of the animals stayed alive? It was a question James Edward Cooper decided might have to be ruled upon in the courts, for he determined not to accept it without a fight.

Without regard for the problems he was creating for his heir, William Clapcott Dean had thought mainly of the comfort and ease of his beloved horses and dogs, determined that they should live in happy retirement to the end of their days. He willed that they 'should be kept in the stables, kennels and buildings which they now occupy and that they should not be worked in the future, but only exercised at the discretion of the Trustees and never be sold'. With compassion for the last days of the horses and ponies he willed that 'whenever my Trustees

William Clapcott Dean had exceptional love for his cattle, dogs and horses, both saddle horses and those trained for the plough, like this team pictured here. He left money for his horses to be maintained in happy retirement to the end of their days.
(Photo: HAMPSHIRE MUSEUM SERVICE)

consider that any one of the said horses should be killed, the same shall be shot with a double barrelled gun, both barrels loaded at the same time with clean barrels and a full charge ...' He also bequeathed to the Trustees for 50 years 'if any of the horses, ponies or hounds shall so long live' the cottage and garden then occupied by his groom, William Vatter, as well as the stables, kennels and buildings with the yards adjoining.

How James Edward Cooper responded to these provisions so much in the trustees' favour — possibly the result of pressure put upon William Clapcott Dean during his last two or three weeks alive — we shall shortly see, but as the reading of the will went on, he next heard the dead man remembering those men and women near to him, for a list of legacies amounting to £7,730 (about £270,000 in 1986) and annuities amounting to £2,082 (about £72,800 in 1986) followed. Inevitably, the RSPCA received the largest legacy, of £2,000.

To the two elder brothers of James Edward he bequeathed £1,000 each, the same sum each to his two executors and trustees, Stevens and Chislett, and to four of his own relations, the Clapcotts, annuities of from £400 to £600 a year. To Charles Gifford, partner of his recently deceased surveyor, Christopher Creeke, he left £200, and to Henry Stokes, his helpful manager at the Wiltshire and Dorset Bank, £150. A mysterious lady, Marion Oakley, about whom we do not even know whether she was married or a spinster, was left £150. Who was she, and what was his relationship with her? William Clapcott Dean kept it a secret.

To a brick manufacturer, John Hunt, he left £50, then several legacies to his personal servants and employees. To Eva Harvey, whom he refers to in his will as 'my servant', £20 in addition to her wages; to George Young, his groom, £10 in addition to his wages, to William Vatter, another groom, £10, then £10 each to his gardener, Charles Tanner, his gamekeeper, Edwin Flitten and his foreman, John King. He remembered Lucy Plowman, 'widow of my late gamekeeper, Henry Plowman', and gave her a life annuity of £13 a year and the additional security of four rooms to be chosen by her for use during her life in Towns End Cottage, on the Littledown Estate.

In another act of kindness, he bequeathed 'to my faithful

shepherd, John Clare' an annuity of £13 a year, the use for life of the cottage where he then lived, as well as the cottage and garden at Great Dean then occupied by his gamekeeper, Edwin Flitten. To his cook, Rebecca West, he bequeathed a life annuity of £30 a year in addition to her wages, but he had even warmer feelings for her daughter, Mary West, to whom he left £50 a year for life, and her wages. In his last moments, he thought of William Vivian, a labourer at Littledown, to whom he bequeathed an annuity for life of £26 in a late codicil, four days before he died. This he signed by making his mark, because he was by then so weak. Very touching is this image of William Clapcott Dean thinking on his deathbed not of himself, but the welfare of his humblest workman.

When the implications of the will were explained, James Edward Cooper learned that he had inherited the Dean fortune upon two conditions. First, like his predecessor, he had within a year to 'take upon himself and use in all deeds and writings which he shall sign, and upon all occasions, the surname and arms of Dean either together with or in lieu of his own family surname' — or forfeit the inheritance in favour of the next in line. [There were then no arms; they had to be granted.]

William Clapcott Dean had thus tried to perpetuate the family name for all time, little knowing that three or four generations hence the Dean family would vanish, owing to a failure to marry and procreate. Consequently, his second condition, that 'the person for the time being entitled to the actual possession ... of the said premises ... shall reside at my Littledown house and occupy the same and the farms as now occupied by me' would also come to nothing.

Having heard the will in detail, the three Cooper brothers no doubt wondered why James, the youngest, had inherited the estate. Why had William Clapcott Dean chosen him? They may have found the answer, but we cannot and may only speculate. Perhaps, quite simply, he had taken a liking to him. Or, perhaps, he saw in James a successful and practical businessman more likely than either of his two brothers to manage the estates with care and ability.

One theory about it must be demolished. David Young, author of the detailed history *The Story of Bournemouth*, has deposited notes in the Lansdowne Public Library there, saying that James Edward Cooper succeeded to the estate 'because he would appear to have been the first legitimate child of the Joseph Cooper-Elizabeth Dean marriage'. He quotes as supposed evidence for this an entry in the *Hampshire Allegations for Marriage Licences Granted by the Bishop of Winchester, 1689-1837,* volume 1, page 187: 'Cooper, Joseph, of Holdenhurst, 21, b., and Elizabeth Dean, of the same, 21 sp., at Holdenhurst, 26 May, 1832. Aff.'

He adds: 'Only the Affidavit is in the Bishop's Registry, which suggests that the application may not have been followed up — possibly through opposition of the Dean family — and that the marriage did not take place until a few years later by the more usual process of banns. James Edward would appear to have been the first legitimate child.'

The facts refute this theory entirely and it is hard to understand why David Young advanced it. Holdenhurst Parish Registry records: 'Joseph Cooper and Elizabeth Dean, both of Holdenhurst, married at Holdenhurst by Licence on 28 May 1832. Witnesses, Jane Dean, Edward Cooper, Richard Dean.' The Registry also records the birth of Joseph Cooper, on 28 June 1833, William, 28 February 1835 and James Edward, 18 January 1840. So there is no question of James Edward's elder brothers being illegitimate, and William Clapcott Dean's likely motives in leaving the bulk of his fortune to James Edward Cooper, the youngest son, remain unexplained.

Before leaving York, to reside at Littledown House, James Edward tried to obtain from Walter Rawlins some knowledge of the degree of control over the Dean Estates that the trustees, Stevens and Chislett, would attempt to impose during their year of control. He also wished to know how far he could legally venture in opposing anything they wished to do that he found not to his liking. He received the opinion that it would be unwise of them to insist upon a literal interpretation of the clause in the will to the effect that for a year they should have sole control.

Walter Rawlins pushed the issue a stage further by informing Chislett of his opinion. No doubt to his surprise he was rebuffed for his pains, and he informed James Edward accordingly: 'We have seen Mr Chislett this morning,' he said, in a letter on 19 December 1887, 'and we gave him our opinion as to the trustees term of one year as we gave you, but we find that both he and Dr Stevens intend to keep sole control over all matter for the term. He told us that it was Mr Clapcott Dean's expressed wish to both of them, that this should be so.'

Faced with this disagreeable prospect, James Cooper began to wind up his business affairs in York and, with the trustees' gracious permission, made ready to take up residence in Littledown with his wife Anna, his two daughters, Alice and Ellen, and Joseph, his son, then aged 21. He also instructed Walter Rawlins to have his name changed by Royal Licence to James Edward Cooper Dean, which process they began at the College of Arms.

The sudden transformation from businessman to land magnate, James Edward Cooper seems to have taken in his stride. In one of his old account books, listing orders for minor things like repairs to the roof at a vicarage in York, and carpentering a range of cupboards elsewhere, we find him practising his new signature of James Cooper Dean, which grew larger, more flowing and confident at each attempt. His portrait in oils, painted almost life-size when he was in his fifties, shows a handsome, well-groomed man of Edwardian appearance in a brown homburg hat with a pink rose in the lapel of his fashionably cut fawn-coloured suit. There is a thrust to his chin above the well-combed beard, a humorous twinkle in his sharp blue eyes. He carries in a somewhat dandified manner a silver-topped cane, but clearly he is a dandy with his feet on the ground.

Such a man was not to be over-ridden by William Clapcott Dean's trustees, and friction over relatively minor matters forecast conflict. Early in January, Chislett wrote to him saying that all William Clapcott Dean's numerous ledgers, records and papers should be destroyed or otherwise disposed of. Quick to resent this, James replied sharply: 'You will oblige me by leaving everything whatever as regards ledgers, etc., as Mr Dean left them and nothing must be either destroyed or removed — that is my wish!' It was a minor victory for him, but there were other clashes, big and small, to come. Later in

January, before he took up residence, he gave instructions for the employment of some of the servants there who had little work to do to be terminated. Chislett promptly counter-manded these orders and told Walter Rawlins that the servants were to be kept on — at James Cooper's expense. 'Under these circumstances we see no help for it,' Rawlins lamented.

Nevertheless, early in March 1888, when James had moved into Littledown, Rawlins felt the time had come to explain to the trustees as clearly as possible exactly what were their powers under the will. First, he explained, as executors, their duties were simply to pay the testator's debts, if any, pay the expenses of probate and the winding up of this portion of the Estate and then to pay the residue to the residuary legatee, Mr Cooper. Although the law gave a year for this, there was little reason, he said, why they should not complete this and pay over the residue to Mr Cooper during the present month, or pay over as much as they could safely do, leaving about £1,000 in the bank until the estate was finally wound up.

Evidently Dr Stevens was keeping James Edward waiting for money that he needed now that he was no longer in busi-ness, so Walter Rawlins advised him: 'You must remember that as executors, having paid the debts and expenses and lega-cies your only liability is to the residuary legatee [James Cooper] and you cannot be wrong if you dispose of the residue or any part of it under his written directions. If Dr Stevens does not like to pay the fees on the change of name out of the personality, then you should clearly, and we say this without any doubt, pay over as much as you can of the residue to the residuary legatee and he can pay the fees. This latter is the best course undoubtedly, as it is not fair to keep the principal lega-tee waiting, having paid all the others.'

Pointing out that as tenant for life James could, subject to their consent, deal with the property as he desired during their year in charge of it, Rawlins emphasised that he was entitled to receive the rents from the estate, but the trustees need not ac-tually pay them to him, unless they thought proper.

James Edward Cooper, cousin of William Clapcott Dean, was obliged to change his name to Cooper Dean when he inherited the property fortune. He gave generously to Bournemouth throughout his life. (Photo: MORRIS BENJAMIN)

The Prince of Wales, later King Edward, (background left) finds time in this Illustrated London News drawing to stroll through Bournemouth's Lower Pleasure Gardens during his visit in 1890 to open the Royal Victoria Hospital on the site given by William Clapcott Dean.

Regarding the further development for housing in Bournemouth, he said that James wished to let some of the land with the legitimate object of increasing his income 'but unless you as trustees are in the agreements the land cannot be entered upon during the year and anyone who commenced building without your consent expressed in the agreement would be liable to have his building stopped at any time...

'So long as James Cooper ... signs the agreements you cannot incur any responsibility to anyone. He has a legal right to

let out the land as tenant for life and there can be no possible
object in your refusing to assign your term ... As a matter of
fact ... we got our conveyancing counsel to approve and settle
the agreements and any leases there may be for your execu-
tion, so that you practically have the benefit of counsel's
opinion that you are acting right in doing what Mr Cooper
asks you to do.'

Clearly, Rawlins feared that the trustees' reluctance to co-
operate could adversely affect development of the estates, and
of Bournemouth. By now, the projected Victoria Hospital site
needed either to be donated in accordance with William
Clapcott Dean's wishes or, should James Cooper so desire, be
cancelled. In the first test of his goodwill he generously reconveyed the land to the new hospital's trustees, Stevens and

125

Chislett having raised no objection. Designed in the Queen Anne style by the Christopher Creeke and Charles Gifford partnership, it was built by the firm of George & Harding and was officially opened on 16 January 1890 by the Prince of Wales before his succession as King Edward VII. But of William Clapcott Dean, whose original gift of land made the hospital possible, or James Edward Cooper, who, while still a stranger to the Bournemouth community, had willingly given the land anew, no mention was recorded upon or in the building; no bust, portrait or commemorative plaque.

But despite his humble social status in class-conscious Victorian England, James Edward Cooper had shown that he was a man of metal, someone not to be pushed around. Having taken up residence at Littledown in February 1888, leaving for good the noise and bustle of building in the city of York for its quiet green acres, doubtless for the first time he comprehended the real and extraordinary extent of his inheritance — Carew's and Pigshoot farms, apart from Littledown; numerous cottages, a fortune in cash and securities, as well as the extensive Dean Park and West Cliff estates in the aspiring new seaside town. Few men can have experienced such a sudden and dramatic change of fortune, formally sealed with his change of name by Royal Licence to James Edward Cooper Dean, on 2 June 1888, and announced in the *London Gazette* of 15 June 1888.

Meantime, the trustees, both ambitious men, informed James Cooper Dean that they intended to claim the horses' and hounds' £750 annuity without giving any account of their expenditure. It was a blunt statement of their claim over 50 years to this large sum of money, and on top of their 12 months' lordship of the estates it was too much. With legal advice, James threatened to contest the issue. They refused to give way; counsel were briefed and the case was set down for Hearing. It came up in the Chancery Division of the High Court on 30 March, then 4 and 9 April 1889.

James Cooper Dean sought a declaration that the gift of £750 a year to the defendants was invalid; or, alternatively, a declaration that he himself was entitled under the will to the balance from time to time in any year after provision by the trustees for the maintenance of the horses, hounds, stables and kennels. Mr Cozens Hardy, Q.C., and Mr Vernon Smith appeared for James Cooper Dean, and Mr Everitt, Q.C. and Mr Alexander for the defendants.

Mr Cozens Hardy argued that the testator, William Clapcott Dean, never intended that the £750 should be in any way applied to the benefit of the trustees personally, and that the plaintiff, James Cooper Dean, was entitled to the surplus income. Mr Everitt argued, on the contrary, that the £750 a year was a distinct gift to the defendants, and that its expenditure was left entirely to their discretion.

In Mr Justice North's view the first question was whether the whole trust was invalid — because neither horses, nor dogs, could enforce it! Is there, he questioned, with perplexed solemnity, 'anything illegal or obnoxious to the law in the nature of the provision — that is, in the fact that it is not for human beings, but for horses and dogs?'

It was a startling question. The whole court waited breathlessly for the shafts of erudition and logic that would throw light upon this impenetrable problem — namely, because neither a horse nor a dog could enforce it, was the trust invalid? In his opinion, said Justice North, mercifully relaxing the tension that gripped the court, it was not. He quoted a case in British India in 1850 in which the will of an English officer who had left the sum of £1,800 to the Government of Bengal for the maintenance of his large stable of horses, was challenged. The case had dragged on for eleven years, and two only of the horses were still alive, but the verdict, on behalf of the ultimate defendant, Lord Auckland, Governor-General of India, established clearly the validity of the provision in favour of the two remaining horses. So, pronounced Mr Justice North, while it was undoubtedly true that the horses and hounds in this case could not enforce the trust themselves, it was still perfectly legal.

But, he went on, getting to grips with the issue, the question was whether the annuity was given to the trustees 'beneficially', that is for their own benefit. 'In my opinion, he declared shortly, 'it was not given to them beneficially ... If the testator had meant them to take beneficially it would have been very easy to say that "any surplus after satisfying the aforesaid purposes shall be divided among them for their own use". But the testator said nothing of the sort...

'It is clear, therefore, that he was considering the benefit of the animals which are the object of the trust, and *prima facie* it was not his intention to benefit the trustees as distinct from the animals....

'It is clear that he was not leaving the trustees a discretion as to the way in which they were to deal with the animals, but he was giving directions as to what was to be done about them ... and not merely giving them an absolute discretion to apply the money to those purposes or to any other purpose they pleased..

'I must, therefore, declare that the trustees do not take the surplus beneficially; but upon the question whether the surplus belongs to their heir-at-law or to the devisee of the real estate ... I say nothing, in the absence of the heir-at-law.'

So, the trustees were fully accountable for the expenditure, and the surplus went to James Cooper Dean, as the devisee, the judge not having pronounced as to its disposal. It was a satisying, though expensive start to James Cooper Dean's reign over the estates. By the end of 1888 the tight-fisted lordship of Dr Stevens and Mr Chislett had come to an end, and only in their stewardship over the animals at Littledown did he occasionally sight them.

Much at home in the field of building and housing development, James looked forward to running the estates more profitably, with the help of Charles Gifford, who still managed the architect and surveyor's office, but he very quickly became aware of the obstacles that stood in the way of this. The estates covered more than 1,000 acres, and before building sites there could be offered for sale he himself was obliged to finance out of his income the entire cost of making roads, drains and sewers. It was a huge and costly undertaking and he soon found he was spending much of his income upon it. This clashed with his firm belief that since these expenses were for the benefit of the estates not only at that time, but in the future, the cost should be borne by the estates, not by himself alone, as the tenant for life.

His income in 1890 apart from his investment income, amounted to about £15,330, mainly from the sale during the 27 years since 1863 when they started, of a total of 2,190 building sites in Bournemouth with an average annual ground rent of £7. Farming at Littledown and elsewhere showed losses, for a second phase of the great agricultural depression that had started in Britain in 1875 had begun in 1890 to consign the industry to rack and ruin nation-wide owing to huge imports of frozen meat from Australia and New Zealand, grain from the United States. Yet he was paying for the erection of new farm buildings and cottages, as well as the maintenance of existing ones on the Littledown estate and repairs to the house itself, for by nature and training it was James Cooper Dean's practice to improve wherever possible.

Apart from this, he had become anxious about the future of his two unmarried daughters, Alice and Ellen, both in their mid-twenties and living somewhat solitary lives, for Anna, his wife, had died through illness soon after their arrival at Littledown. To provide for them presented a problem, because under William Clapcott Dean's will the estates were held by him for life, then after his death, by his son Joseph, and

Westover Pleasure Grounds, bordered by trees and within sight and sound of the sea, symbolised Bournemouth's prized tranquility. James Cooper Dean contended that a proposed private tramway service would destroy this unique atmosphere and therefore opposed permission for it.

subsequently, his sons. Might it be possible, he asked himself, to have the terms of the will altered so that capital could be more easily raised to cover these various objects?

It was an issue upon which he decided to seek legal advice in due course, but meantime in 1890 his anger was aroused by a private company's attempt to obtain authority from the Board of Trade to launch a tramway service from Poole along the Poole Road to the centre of Bournemouth through the northern boundary of his West Cliff estate. Tramways, with their noisy crash of metal upon metal as they thundered along steel tracks banging bells defiantly, were generally held at that time to lower the values of any good quality houses past which they ran.

He formally objected to the scheme in March 1890 in a letter to the licencing authority, the Board of Trade, on the above grounds; secondly, that the trams would cause traffic obstruction along the Poole Road, a mere 44 feet wide, and finally that the London & South Western Railway were intending to open a station opposite the Branksome Park estate for the convenience of people living along the route of the proposed tramway. His, and other similar objections made the scheme's financial backers hesitate, until finally they abandoned it, although of course the Bournemouth municipality established its own comprehensive tramways system in the borough in 1902.

Nevertheless, James Cooper Dean was satisfied in having been instrumental in obstructing the scheme as first proposed. His main concern during the last years of the century was the profitable development of the Bournemouth estates; another 860 building sites were sold from 1891 to 1896, with average annual ground rents of £10. But the financial outlay upon road making had become too heavy, and he determined upon a legal re-settlement of the estates, both for this reason, and because, at the age of 55, he had surprisingly, formed a romantic attachment, and was thinking of marrying again.

CHAPTER 9

No Marriage

IN HIS MID-FIFTIES in 1895, hale, hearty, handsome, a widower and wealthy, James Cooper Dean was an attractive matrimonial target for any of the merry widows of standing in Bournmouth left alone by officer-husbands who had gone to early graves in England's colonial wars in Africa, Afghanistan, Burma, China or India.

About the lady he wished to marry, we know nothing except that she was a widow with a family of young children for whom she was anxious to provide; but one may speculate. Was she fair or dark, tall, graceful and attractive, or round and tubby. We can guess that she would have been good to look at, for physical beauty of all kinds attracted James Cooper Dean. And, no doubt, bright and sociable, too. By the Spring of 1895, he had evidently become fond enough of her to propose marriage, despite the encumbrance — if it could so be called — of her young family. And evidently his proposal had been accepted, though no trace of any notice of engagement or forthcoming wedding ceremony can be found in the public press of the time. But we do know that he had agreed to provide a substantial sum for her children's education and upbringing, as well as to make a settlement in her favour to take effect upon his death. So this was one reason why James Edward wished to arrange a re-settlement of the Estates upon less rigid terms.

The other was, of course, his continued costly investment in road-making in the West Cliff and Dean Park Estates. Bournemouth, which had received its charter of incorporation as a municipal borough in 1890, continued to attract new residents eager to purchase leases of building sites, and the value

Military bands, heralds, tableaux and citizens on foot and horseback follow the bearer of Bournemouth's charter of incorporation on 27 August 1890 in a procession to the pier, where it was read aloud in his stentorian voice by James Druitt, clerk to the town Commissioners. The document had been dispatched from London by rail by the Privy Council. (Illustrated London News)

of the Estates grew all the time, for the town was no longer only a genteel resort for rich and elderly invalids.

With the arrival of better railway communications and the birth of cultural and sporting facilities, its status among seaside towns grew like a golden halo in the 1890s. The railway line from Christchurch was extended through the Dean Park estate to Bournemouth West, and the Central Station was opened in 1885. The Royal Victoria Hospital provided the town with an up-to-date infirmary for the sick and injured; a municipal orchestra, directed by Dan Godfrey jnr., played in the Winter Gardens, leading by 1895 to regular symphony concerts given by the newly formed Municipal Orchestra — the first of its kind in the country, today known as the Bournemouth Symphony and Symphonia Orchestras. Professional repertory companies performced in the Theatre Royal, erected in Albert Road at a cost of £10,000 and managed by Harry Nash, but enlarged, and re-named the Bournemouth Theatre and Opera House in 1892.

The commercial libraries apart, a public library under the direction of Mr Charles Riddle opened at No. 6 Cumnor Terrace in January 1895, with a reading room at Boscombe. Primary and secondary education were provided in numerous private and state schools. Sport of almost every variety attracted young and old, the facilities at hand including a municipal golf links from 1894, the Dean Park Cricket Ground, several bowling greens, a rifle range and shooting club, football at the Dean Court Football ground, near Thistlebarrow Road. Let at a nominal rent by James Cooper Dean to the original Boscombe Athletic Football Club, it later became the Bournemouth and Boscombe Athletic Football Club, of which he became vice-president.

All this was a far cry from the cultural and social ghost-town that had so dismayed Grantley Berkeley in 1860, and it became possible mainly owing to the growth of population and commerce in the town, the arrival of younger, more active people with a penchant for new ideas in place of the ultra-conservative and invalid mentality that had characterised it in the past. During the years 1881 to 1891, the population had more than doubled from 16,859 to 37,650, with a corresponding growth in the town's rateable value up to £261,213. To a large extent, this increase was due also to the greater area of the new borough, which, spreading from 1,643 acres in 1841 to 2,592 in 1891, naturally attracted more trade and more poeple, but the endless influx of residents drawn by Bournemouth's appeal as a beautiful place in which to live was no less a potent factor.

Throughout the Dean Estates, by 1890, so far as can be ascertained, a total of some 430 building sites with an average ground rent of £12 yearly had been leased, bringing James

Overleaf:
Domestic staff and farm workers at Littledown House pose in their Sunday best, with straw hats and babies, for this group photograph taken about 1890. Included are game-keeper William Vatter, groom Henry Vivian, steward John King, housekeeper Elizabeth Fisher and cook Mary-Ann Vivian.

James Cooper Dean and friend set off for a day's shooting in his four-wheeled wagonette. The Littledown estate was well-stocked with game, including pheasant, partridge, woodcock, quail and hares.

Cooper Dean an annual income of £5,160 gross, but from this he was obliged to fund the heavy costs of road-making and of administration. Having regard to the value of the estates it evidently seemed a nonsense to him that he should be unable to provide more generously for his son Joseph and his two daughters, Alice and Ellen. The terms of William Clapcott Dean's will, entailing the estates for future generations, offended against his businessman's belief in ready access to available capital.

But it would be absurd to give the impression that he was hard up. Certainly he had been obliged both to spend his income and to draw on the cash and securities that he had inherited, but he was still a very rich man. He could afford luxuries that he would hardly have dreamed of owning in his earlier life in York. He had built up a fine stable of horses, among which were five or six hunters, two or three ponies and several harness horses for his collection of carriages. These included a four-wheeled, closed four-seater brougham; a two-seater four-wheeled victoria with a raised seat in front for the driver; a four-wheeled landau with a folding roof; a small, elegant cabriolet for two with a collapsible hood, a two-seater chaise and a light four-wheeled wagonette. With their shining harness and immaculately groomed horses, these equipages drew admiring glances as their owner trotted them along the Westover Road.

Nor did he lack willing hands at Littledown. Apart from 12 farm-workers, his steward John King, his gamekeeper William Vatter, his groom Henry Vivian, and their several helpers ran the farm, while his housekeeper, Elizabeth Fisher, his cook, Mary-Ann Vivian and their underlings, managed Littledown House. He was also able to indulge his enjoyment in shooting. A crack shot, he had been awarded a silver tea service and a silver cup as first prizes in two celebrated contests. His gamekeeper kept the lands well-stocked with every species of game bird, including in season pheasant, woodcock, partridge and snipe. The plentiful game and his reputation as a crack shot attracted eminent guests to his shooting parties in the knowlege that the day would be well spent. A photograph of an eccentric landowner and sportsman of the day, Sir Francis Dashwood, seated with James Cooper Dean in a four-in-hand, still survives. The gunroom at Littledown House held a row of

Sir Francis and Lady Dashwood, and James Cooper Dean (centre) depart from Littledown House on a tour of the estate. Shooting was their common interest and both men were said to be crack shots.

In a modest two-wheeler, one of his collection of carriages, James Cooper Dean sets off for a visit to the estate offices in Bournemouth.

gleaming guns, from which he chose according to his fancy and the weather. After the first year in the house he began improving the gardens there with flowers and flowering shrubs, creating the fine long avenues of rhododendrons and azaleas that blazed purple, white and scarlet in early summer.

One of his main interests at home was reading, mainly contemporary novels, to judge by the contents of his library. Among other works arguing an active mind on the shelves of his Georgian mahogany bookcases were 30 leather-bound volumes of the works of Charles Dickens, 48 volumes of Sir Walter Scott's works, 12 volumes of the novelist Smollett, six volumes of Alexandre Dumas and 18 of George Meredith's novels, as well as a number of books relating to agriculture, horses and stock breeding. From time to time he made available several acres of land for the Royal Counties agricultural shows.

Nor, on inheriting Littledown House, had he to acquire furniture, for it had been copiously furnished by its successive occupants during the past century with fine 17th and 18th century mahogany pieces. And he had no need for the time being to replenish the cellar; its racks were abundantly stocked

Haymaking, with scythe and pitchfork was a bi-annual chore on the lush pastures surrounding Littledown House, now covered by streets of newly-built houses.

with fine wines, Napoleon brandy, whiskies and liqueurs. He entertained little, except for shooting or card parties, playing whist or poker with men and women friends sometimes to the early hours. A country lover, he was said to be happiest out walking round the Littledown estate, when, accompanied by a friend and followed by one or more of his dogs, he could chat with his workers about the progress of the crops and inspect his sheep, pigs and cattle on the nearby pastures. Thus, he had adapted to his new life of Victorian country gentleman with remarkable ease; and to his status as land magnate with good sense and practical intelligence.

So it was only the entailments in William Clapcott Dean's will as they affected his proposed re-marriage; the provision for his son Joseph and for his own two daughters, plus the cost of the necessary road making on the estates that caused ripples of concern to marr the well-ordered serenity of his days. By the mid-1890, Alice and Ellen, both then in their late twenties and still residing at Littledown, seemed unlikely ever to marry, so he decided to provide a secure future in the material sense for both of them. Yet with the estates entailed, he could provide neither for them nor, effectively, for Joseph while he himself was alive; and meantime, following the family tradition, Joseph contemplated marriage with his cousin, Bethia Cooper.

Having hesitated about seeking a re-settlement of the estates for five or six years, James at last turned in May 1895 for advice to Thomas Rawlins (son of Walter) of the legal firm Rawlins and Rawlins, of Wimborne, who promptly consulted Mr R.J. Pitfield, of 3 Grays Inn Square, London, the Counsel upon whom they relied in such cases. He, in turn, sounded Mr A.W. Rowden, an eminent Counsel learned in the field of estate re-settlement. And in a letter dated 25 May 1895 Mr Rowden stated that the terms of William Clapcott Dean's will could be changed through a Re-settlement Deed, provided that James Cooper Dean's own son, Joseph, understood clearly that he was in no way obliged to agree to this change, since it would involve his parting with absolute control of the estates after his father's death. In a word, his agreement must be voluntary.

But regarding James Cooper Dean's proposed re-marriage with the un-named lady, Mr Rowden advised against making provision in the proposed deed. 'Simply let Mr Cooper Dean insure his life adequately,' he advised, 'so that should he die before her the lady will receive a sum big enough to maintain her in comfort for the rest of her life.' This alone evidently did not satisfy the needs and hopes of his intended new wife. She asked for something more substantial and immediate, money that she could spend upon her children's education directly she became Mrs James Cooper Dean. And to this, James Edward agreed, whether whole-heartedly, or owing to persuasion and argument, we do not know, but it would seem to be a request hard to refuse, on the verge of matrimony. He instructed Thomas Rawlins jnr. to include in the Re-settlement Deed a jointure of £500 a year for her after his death and the generous sum of £15,000 immediately upon their marriage, for the upbringing and education of her children, the family to reside with him, of course, at Littledown House.

Everything was agreed, these particular arrangements were duly written as clause 13 in Mr. A.W. Rowden's legal summary of the Re-settlement Deed of 24 May 1895. Then, at the last moment, an unexplained obstacle arose to stop the marriage. A thick line in black ink was drawn through the clause to which it referred in the Deed summary. A marriage that could have saved the Cooper Dean family from extinction had mysteriously come to nought.

What happened to prevent this marriage so important to James Cooper Dean that he was willing to bestow more money upon his intended wife than upon his own daughers and son? Once again, we can only speculate. There are no letters or other documentary evidence to throw light upon the mystery. Did Joseph object to so expensive a proposed marriage and refuse, unless his father broke it off, to give his legal agreement to the proposed Re-settlement Deed? It is known that father and son were estranged from about this date; and Joseph, having married his cousin, Bethia Cooper, moved out of Littledown and away to Southsea, 36 Victoria Road. So it is a possible explanation.

However, the problem of the hoped-for marriage having been unhappily disposed of, the Re-settlement Deed was drafted and signed on 13 June 1898 by James, his son Joseph, his cousin, James Cooper, and solicitor Walter Rawlins, as trustees. A document running to some 9,000 words, it covered all possible legal contingencies and financial arrangements in favour of the beneficiaries, their children and children's children for the next 1,000 years.

Among its most significant features were, first, James Edward Cooper Dean to retain his life interest in the Estates: the entailment in favour of his son Joseph was barred, although upon his father's death, Joseph, in turn, would inherit a life interest, and after him, his children. Expenditure upon roads and other improvements were henceforward to be chargeable to the Estates through the sale of land and property, rather than to James Cooper Dean's income from them.

With traditional Dean generosity, the Deed also authorised the sale for a 'nominal consideration' of pieces of land not exceeding five acres as sites for any place of religion, parsonage house, burial ground, school house, residence of a school master or mistress, school playground, public museum, library, town hall or other public building; or for baths, wash-houses, lecture or reading rooms. James Cooper Dean kept bright the flame of benevolence first lit by William Clapcott Dean.

In return for his co-operation in this legal re-settlement, Joseph received an income of £400 a year and the sum of £10,000, as well as a life interest in the estates upon his father's death, to be inherited by his son or daughters and their children, in turn. James Cooper Dean's daughters, Alice and Ellen, received £13,333 6s 8d each, and annuities of £450, to be raised by mortgage, or by the sale of timber. For Joseph's wife, his cousin Bethia Cooper, the Deed authorised a settlement of £300 a year upon Joseph's death, so long as she remained a widow, to be increased to £1,000 a year upon the death of her father-in-law, again so long as she was a widow.

James Cooper Dean had thus succeeded in providing generously for his family, while making money available from the estates for housing development. He was able under certain conditions to sell small areas of the estates, through which the Council and the town were soon to benefit. Following its known policy of increasing the number of open spaces for public pleasure gardens and recreation grounds in the town, the Council approached him with an offer to buy or lease the 14 acres of wild land called, owing to its shape, Horseshoe

Common, separated by Dean Park Road and Cavendish Road from the Dean Park cricket ground.

Negotiations led to an agreement whereby the Corporation bought two acres of the Common for £8,000 and leased a further 12 acres for 99 years from September 1896, at a nominal annual rent of £5. The Corporation intended to use the two-acre site fronting the Old Christchurch Road for erecting municipal office buildings, subject to ending (with compensation) the restrictive covenants in a number of leases granted by William Clapcott Dean on houses around the Horseshoe. These covenants prohibited buildings except a gardener's lodge and an estate office on any part. The Corporation agreed that within 21 years from the date for the erection of any municipal buildings they should provide the Dean Estate with an eight-room suite of offices there; and before erecting any municipal buildings they should submit the designs to James Cooper Dean for his approval, but the municipal buildings were never put up. The upper part of the Horseshoe was laid out in 1899 as pleasure gardens of a somewhat wild character, which remained even when they were divided by the broad sweep of the Wessex Way, the traffic artery slashed through the town-centre in the 1970s.

Of some interest in this transaction is the £8,000 that James Cooper Dean charged the Corporation for the two acres they had acquired. It was the first time in the history of the Dean Estates' transactions with the Corporation or with trustees representing hospitals, schools and churches, that an ecomonic price for land had been charged. Hitherto, land had been given or leased for a nominal sum, like the 12 acres of the Horseshoe Common at £5 a year. Could it have been that James, a man with a very practical turn of mind, had learned to distinguish between the public good, and the ambitions of local bureaucracy, whose members had shown little if any appreciation of the family's liberality in the past?

Since inheriting the estates, he had tried to maintain a balance between public and personal advantage. For example, having received complaints from residents on the West Cliff estate that local youths were damaging trees and other property there, he wrote offering the land to the Council on certain conditions, for a nominal yearly rent. The Council having conceived attractive development plans for the area which had some years before been frustrated by William Clapcott Dean, was willing. In 1901, a formal agreement was drawn up, which, for its historical interest, is worth reading: 'For the benefit of the inhabitants of Bournemouth generally the said James Edward Cooper Dean . . . doth hereby dedicate all those several strips of land . . . situate on the West Cliff estate . . . known as the West Overcliff Drive. And the two roads from the West Cliff Road to the parts where they respectively communicate with the Overcliff Drive . . . Also the Middle Chine bridge.

'To the end and intent that the same Overcliff Drive Roads and bridges may respectively for ever . . . become part of the Public Highways and be used and engaged by the public accordingly.' The Council were also authorised to build and maintain a bridge over Durley Chine and a bridge over Alum Chine for pedestrians and bath-chairs only.

The Council accepted a 999-year-lease of the Middle Chine and a lease of the land on the Plateau, between Middle and Alum Chines, containing one acre and three roods, at an annual rent of £105, reducible to £5 5s on the observance of the condition that the land should be kept as an open space. In addition, it accepted a 999-year-lease of the land and cliff on the outer side of the Overcliff Drive at £400 a year, reducible

An 1865 engraving by an unknown artist shows part of the West Cliff area leased to the borough council in 1901 for 999 years at a nominal rent by James Cooper Dean 'for the benefit of the inhabitants of Bournemouth...'

to £10 a year on observance of the condition not to build on the land, or to convert it into an Undercliff Drive.

The Council then went ahead with laying out the Argyle Pleasure Gardens on two acres of land provided by James Cooper Dean for a nominal rent, and the construction of the West Overcliff Drive. When completed, the latter extended for a mile from Durley Chine on the east to Alum Chine on the west, winding past the pine trees along the western bank of Durley Chine, inland beside the eastern side of Middle Chine, to traverse the upper part of the gorse-covered Chine over an ornamental iron bridge, then continuing by the western bank of Middle Chine and the Cliff front in sight of the sea, with a final inland turn along the eastern bank of Alum Chine.

The official opening of this beautiful new drive, first planned for 16 October 1902, took place on 6 November, with much civic ceremonial. James Cooper Dean handed over the deeds with a formal dedication to the Mayor, Councillor G. Frost. Having declared the Drive open for the enjoyment and use of the public, the Mayor adjourned with other local functionaries for the enjoyment of a luncheon given by James at Bourne Hall. Altogether, the Council spent £15,233 in laying out the Pleasure Gardens and constructing the Drive. Had it not been for James Cooper Dean's generosity in providing the land at a nominal price the cost of this achievement would, of course, have been much greater.

A keen sense of civic duty and of generosity towards his fellow citizens seems to have motivated this *nouveau riche* but kind-hearted land magnate. Like William Clapcott Dean before him he invariably listened to appeals for land for constructive purposes. Apart from the arrangements to which we have already referred, in 1891 he found a site for a Baptist Church in Lansdowne Road, Westborne, for 99 years at a nominal rent; and for the proposed St. Ambrose's Church of England church he gave outright in 1896 the valuable freehold site on West Cliff Road, where the church still stands. But no less than the needs of religion, those arising from Victorian England's colonial wars and military accomplishments touched him. In 1896, during the years of the South African Wars, he provided land at a nominal rent of £5 5s a year on a 99-years-lease for the Royal Artillery Volunteers' drill hall, and a site for the 7th Battalion the Hampshire Regiment's drill hall for 99 years at £5 a year.

One of his keenest interests was the welfare of local children, which led to his becoming a member of the governing board of the local branch of the Cottage Homes for Children, and to this charity (similar to Dr Barnado's Homes) he gave financial help to improve the children's lives and conditions. The Homes ran Boy Scouts and Girl Guides troops, once staging a special parade which he attended. He described this event as one of the happiest sights that he had seen in Bournemouth for years.

A lover of sports and athletics, he was an occasional member of the Holdenhurst cricket eleven, also a familiar figure in his white straw hat, white flannels and blazer at matches on the Dean Park ground, especially during the Bournemouth Cricket Festival held there. President of the club, he gave a substantial sum of money towards the cost of the fine pavilion erected in 1902.

Though he took a strong and benevolent interest in the town, he liked at the same time to be able to withdraw to the peace and seclusion of his own acres at Littledown. So, when he heard in 1898 that the Iford Estate of nearly 400 acres

Members of the Holdenhurst cricket eleven, with friends, pose for this team photograph in 1902 in the Dean Park cricket ground. Cloth caps or straw hats were equally acceptable.

adjoining Littledown was soon to be auctioned, with large-scale house-building likely to follow on part of the land, he was immediately concerned, but there was a way to stop it. Why should he not buy it himself? There were good reasons to do so.

First, the land included fishing rights and land to shoot over, a big attraction. Secondly, like many big landowners he preferred when he looked over the fields to see his own land and only his own land. The prospect of a suburb of Bournemouth mushrooming on the horizon appalled him. Thirdly, the acquisition of land brought an increase in social prestige, and he by no means lacked appreciation of that. Finally, the land in question was bound to grow in value. He decided to attend the sale.

The catalogue acclaimed the developmental possibilities: 'In view of the rapid and almost complete development of the Eastern extremity of the Borough, this Estate must gradually but surely come into maturity for building operations. It is obviously the only FREEHCLD ESTATE (of any appreciable extent) ON THE MAIN ROAD between Poole and Christchurch REMAINING UNDEVELOPED as a building estate. In addition to the main road frontages, there are other portions of the estate having good road frontages, ripe for building.'

It was this eulogy, this call by the auctioneers to land developers to buy up the land and erect a forest of houses on his borders that finally stirred James Cooper Dean to buy the land himself. But before the sale, due on Thursday, 23 June 1898 at 3 pm, he arranged a walk round the properties to see what he might be buying. Lot One, an early Victorian country house named Iford House, with several bedrooms, servants' rooms and stables standing in 14 acres of land, described as a 'Gentleman's Miniature Country Seat' he decided against, despite its fishing rights. He had no need of another mansion.

Lot 2, Iford Farm, included 352 acres of arable and pasture land, 25 acres of heath and wood lands adjoining, a fine farmhouse with five bedrooms, a large brick and tiled barn, stables, granary, cow and poultry houses, numerous other outbuildings, a six-roomed cottage and two four-roomed thatched cottages with small gardens, with a total annual rental income of £475. The auctioneers declared that it was the 'only undeveloped land with any important frontage on the main road, on the east or west side of Bournemouth'. It was an open invitation to ambitious builders and he decided to acquire it.

Lot 3, an early Victorian Gothic style house known as The Old Vicarage, stood in seven acres of wooded grounds on the summit of Pokesdown Hill, on the borders of the village, with fine views over the valley of the Stour and Avon rivers and the Littledown estate. It possessed five bedrooms, four downstairs rooms, kitchens and pantry, a coach-house with two bedrooms and a living room, stables, a well-planted kitchen-garden and duck pond. James Cooper Dean noted the absence of any bathroom, but observing that this could easily be remedied, he decided, as a gesture of reconciliation, to buy it for his son Joseph, then living at Southsea with his wife and two young daughters.

He also decided to buy a triangular plot of land with a 130-feet frontage on the main road to Southbourne, and another plot of land with six cottages and gardens.

The Iford Estate auction proved to be a major local event. A big crowd of local gentry, of builders and of businessmen from as far away as London turned up at The Mart auction rooms, Old Christchurch Road. Bidding would have been brisk; good quality land for building, for which planning permission was then not of course needed, guaranteed a handsome profit, so it was not certain that he would get what he wanted. He let Lot 1, Iford House, which included little building land, go without a bid, but he determined to use to the full the advantage he possessed for the remainder, Lots 2, 3, 8, 9 and 10, and to bid as high as was necessary. This he did, and the price he paid for the total was £20,105. He wrote a cheque for £2,010 10s as deposit and arranged mortgages for part of the balance.

However, his son Joseph, his wife and their two daughters, evidently did not move at once into the Old Vicarage, for Ellen was born in 1899 and Edith in 1902, both in Victoria Road, Southsea. The discord between father and son seems not, after all, to have healed at the time. Perhaps, as a result, James Cooper Dean grew ever more involved personally in the development of the Dean lands in Bournemouth.

CHAPTER 10

Building Bournemouth

JAMES COOPER DEAN'S purchase of the Iford estate delighted him. A land magnate committed to housing development in the town, he nevertheless appreciated the peace and quiet of the countryside with its rolling pastures, woodlands and fast-flowing rivers. So he regretted the inevitable onward rush of building around Bournemouth and though involved in it himself he sought to keep it at bay where it affected his interests. By now as much a Victorian country gentleman as a Yorkshire businessman, he seems also to have sought to distance himself from some of the changes, both local and national, that he saw occurring around him.

The area of Bournemouth in 1898 comprised 2,593.6 acres with 6,815 inhabited houses and a population officially estimated to have grown since 1891 from 37,650 to 58,280. It was still growing, seaside holidays having become already part of national life, so the town profited commercially with an endless sprouting of small hotels and boarding houses.

Administrative changes affecting Bournemouth's future were also afoot. Influential local people, James Cooper Dean among them, felt that the town deserved the greater status, wider powers and privileges of a County Borough, no less than the legal advantages of its own Court of Quarter Sessions and Commission of Peace. In October 1898 the appropriate 'Memorial Praying To Be Constituted A County Borough' was submitted by the Mayor and Corporation to the Local Government Board. It emphasised that: 'Bournemouth is exclusively a Health and Pleasure Resort — there are no Trades or Manufactures within its area besides the Building and allied trades connected with the growth of the place and those that

149

Horse-drawn transport, as in this photograph of The Square in about 1905, was still the mark of a leisured age in Bournemouth.

supply the wants of the inhabitants. That owing to the character of the town great attention is paid by the Governing Body to sanitary matters, also to the maintenance of Roads, Recreation Grounds, and other Public Places in a high state of efficiency so as to preserve the amenities of the town.'

Pointing out that the borough then formed part of the administrative county of Southampton, being situated in its south-western corner and bounded on the south by the sea, it declared that, looking to its rapid growth and its large rateable value compared with that of the administrative county, its best interests would be served by being constituted a County Borough, with the full self-government that it would bring. The eventual outcome was that Bournemouth was so constituted on 1 April 1900, and henceforward administered by local people. It had come a long way since its birth as a tiny village in the 1840s, a mere 60 years ago.

James Cooper Dean and the Dean Estates were affected by this change in different ways. In August 1901 the new County Borough Council obtained powers to extend its boundaries by 3,257 acres to a total of 5,850 acres through incorporating the urban districts of Pokesdown and Winton, Southbourne parish

150

and part of Holdenhurst parish. The latter contained the future residential estate of Richmond Park, east of Richmond Park Road, part of the Dean Eastwood estate. To deal henceforward with one local authority simplified the development of the Dean Estates.

Secondly, as a result of this new administrative status, James Cooper Dean was appointed a justice of the peace for both county and borough, becoming one of the most regular figures on the bench. Later, he accepted invitations to join the Christchurch Board of Guardians and to stand for the Rural District Council; he was a member of both during the next 20 years. Although a man of great energy, this voluntary work and overseeing the management of the 200 acres of the Littledown estate, inevitably competed for his time with supervising the direction of the Dean Estates. He was able nevertheless, by keeping a watchful eye on the lay-out of roads no less than the style and quality of building, to impress his views regarding development upon those parts of the town under his ownership.

Except for McKinley Road and West Cliff Road, building on the West Cliff estate was nearly completed by 1900, but on the Northwood estate, bounded by Charminster, Iddesleigh, Grafton, St. Luke's and Wimborne Roads; and the Eastwood estate, lying between Queen's Park South Drive and the upper part of Holdenhurst Road, it had hardly begun at the turn of the century, while much of the Dean Park estate had still to be developed. The firm's old brass-bound ledgers for the period show that some 430 plots were leased, mainly for 99 years, with annual ground rents ranging from £40 to £50 on the West Cliff, to as low as £6 on Dean Park, during the ten years from 1900.

But benevolence, as well as business, inspired James Cooper Dean. In November 1900, he leased a two-acre site in Porchester Road to the Council for the nominal rent of £21 a year for 99 years for a secondary school. Far below the market value, it was a concrete expression of his wish to help the growth of state education for children whose parents were unable to pay the cost of private schooling. The well-being of the people of Bournemouth was close to his heart and where this was concerned he was always generous. Two years later, in October

151

1902, he made available to the town parts of the grassy open spaces overlooking the sea on the West Cliff, leasing to the Council for a nominal £50 a year for 99 years first what was known as the Plateau site; then the beautiful Middle Chine, round which the Overcliff Drive curves, for a peppercorn rent of £5 5s a year; and another belt of land beside the Overcliff Drive for 999 years at £10 a year, all conditional upon their remaining public open spaces permanently.

Despite this wide range of responsibilities, he did not forget his own family, lavishing much love and care upon his two unmarried daughters, both then in their late thirties. He was also attached to his cousin, James Cooper, aged 36 in 1903, with whom he shared a passion for shooting. At this time, when he himself was 63 and Alice, Ellen and James Cooper were living with him in Littledown, they agreed together that since his son Joseph was due to inherit the house, Alice and Ellen should have a home of their own, preferably a farm property, with plenty of land, so as to provide a useful income.

Early in 1904 he received details of Stoke Wood House and the adjoining West End House estates, both at Hambledon, 20 miles from Southampton, and about the same distance from Bournemouth. Since he had recently purchased a powerful Napier open touring car, a make then second only to Rolls-Royce, the 40 miles to Hambledon would not inflict an insupportable separation between him and his daugthers.

The two estates, covering 1,745 acres, were offered for sale by the owner, Mr John Alexander Wilson. Stoke Wood House he found to be an attractive eight-bedroom early Victorian country house with gardens, orchards, pasture and paddock, amounting to 23 acres in undulating Hampshire countryside. The estate also included Wallopswood and West End farms, amounting to 1,173 acres of woodland, pasture and farmland; Bushydown Farm, with 395 acres, a farmhouse, six cottages, pasture and arable land, Brooks Farm, with 145 acres and West End House, an attractive Georgian residence in 5½ acres of gardens.

He had surplus funds to invest, for though agriculture had continued to decline owing to the cheap imports from abroad, his income from the Bournemouth estates had risen steeply. Also, he had the vision to realise that, sooner or later, a change of agricultural policy, the coming of motor transport and the consequent urbanisation of much of the countryside would lead to a swing of the pendulum and a rise in land prices. Besides, after a tour of inspection Alice and Ellen were delighted with the prospect of making Stoke Wood House their home.

Negotiations were concluded and contracts for the sale of the different properties were signed on 29 March and 10 October 1904 — except for two of the farms, already let on long leases, and these were acquired several years later, in 1913. During 1904, the two sisters redecorated and furnished the house to their tastes and moved in by the end of the year. What of their lives at Stoke Wood? Neither of them ever married. They lived quietly on the estate, entertaining from time to time and enjoying the management of the farms without their social life ever blossoming. In the class-conscious social climate of the time the Cooper Deans were not accepted as equals by the county's leading families.

James Cooper Dean showed his business acumen at this

Stoke Wood House, Hambledon, some 20 miles from Bournemouth, James Cooper Dean purchased, with nearby West End House, from Mr John Alexander Wilson in 1904, for his daughters Alice and Ellen and his cousin James Cooper.

time by leasing to market gardeners on yearly tenancies land not yet ready for housing development. Bournemouth's ever-growing population had till then to rely mainly on fruit and vegetables brought in from elsewhere, so growers sought land locally for the purpose. Accordingly, James leased to George Wareham 30 acres of land at Rush Corner in 1904 to grow produce wanted for sale in the local greengrocers' shops. Having found a ready market, Wareham leased another 10½ acres, and in 1910 still another 40 acres, to grow more vegetables on land behind Wimborne Road, where Albemarle and Iddesleigh Roads lie today. Other horticulturists followed suit, so that during the next decade much Dean estate land was leased for this purpose on yearly tenancies. Parts of the Northwood and Eastwood estates on the outskirts of the town not yet ready for housing development thus provided income.

In the Eastwood estate he authorised housing development in the years up to 1914 only along the perimeter roads; the Dean Park estate and the remaining roads of the West Cliff estate were already a big enough task. The perimeter roads were Queen's Park South Drive, part of Holdenhurst Road and Richmond Park Road, where the most active builder from 1902 onwards was John Ames Nethercoate. William Scott built a house in Queen's Park South Drive named Bleak House — either the March winds were blowing or he had been enraptured by Charles Dickens' novel. The Meyrick and Queen's Park Golf Club leased from the Dean Estates, land near what is today the Queen's Park roundabout to build a clubhouse overlooking the links. The annual ground rent was £31 10s, but a plaintive note in red ink in the ledger says: 'Only £7 17s 6d collected in December, 1905.'

In the Dean Park estate, James Cooper Dean authorised the sale of plots for houses in Ascham, Charminster, Lansdowne, Lowther, Methuen, Ophir, Porchester, Wellington and Wimborne Roads. A builder named George Henry Rolls built 20 semi-detached houses in Ophir Road in 1901 with the usual

Having fun on Bournemouth pier. Men and women roller skaters enjoy the hurly-burly using the pier as a rink in this lively 1910 drawing by Max Cowper, a local resident. Ankle-length skirts were no handicap. (Illustrated London News)

99-year-leases and ground rents at seven to eight guineas a year. In 1902, John Ames Nethercoate was putting up houses in the newly-laid Wellington Road, while later in 1903/05, Davis & Lambert built nine in Methuen Road and two more in nearby Ascham Road.

In 1906, George Shears & Son built five houses in Porchester Road, where William Hoare erected numbers 31, 33 and 35, having the year before finished two larger ones in McKinley Road, in the West Cliff estate. Frank Brewer, another small builder, was at the same time building numbers 4, 6, 8 and 10 in Lowther Road on the northern boundary on the Dean Park estate.

But progess was slow, at least by present-day standards. A firm named George & Harding were still building in Ascham Road in 1908. The enterprising Mrs Kate Holly, a widow who managed her own building firm, was then finishing two houses in Lowther Road and several in St. Luke's Road. Also at work in Lowther Road were Garnet Ewart Lambert and William Albert Clapcott (possibly a relation of William Clapcott Dean). Houses in Milton Road were first erected in 1910-11 by Walter and Henry Hoare, while Sheare & Son were completing work in Porchester Road after the outbreak of the First World War in 1914. Two houses in St. Luke's Road were finished as late as 1915 and 1917, doubtless by men unfit for military service, but this apart, building during 1914-18 slowed almost to a standstill, neither the Dean Park nor the West Cliff estates being fully built up by 1918.

One is inclined to assess this seemingly slow rate of building by the pace of present-day semi-mechanised construction, but building was then of course an entirely manual operation carried out by small firms with limited capital and few skilled workers. Nevertheless, standards of workmanship were high, under the watchful eye of James Cooper Dean, the land magnate who never forgot his early years as a master builder.

From time to time he used reputedly to drive in his light, two-wheeled chaise, a rose in his lapel, brown homburg hat worn at an angle, to cast an eye over building progress. He was entirely responsible for road names, and his choice of them casts a little light on his interests and beliefs. His admiration for the aristocracy and the peerage is clear in his choice of

Marlborough and Wellington, then Argyle, Grosvenor, Cavendish, Lansdowne, Lonsdale, Milner, Methuen, Porchester and Portarlington. But as he grew older, this seems to have faded, and he turned to the Bible for inspiration. He chose from it St. Luke's, St. Paul's and Ophir Roads. Perhaps he had been influenced by St. Paul's interpretation of Christianity and by the Parables of the Unjust Steward, and of the Sower, in St. Luke's gospel, to the extent that he wished to commemorate them tangibly.

But how came he to choose Ophir, exotic, jewel-like name? He would have discovered it in the Book of Kings. Ophir was reputedly situated on the south-west coast of what is today the Southern Yemen, whose ancient inhabitants, a wealthy people named the Sabaeans, were before the advent of Christianity ruled by the Queen of Sheba. They controlled the sea and caravan routes in gold and other precious commodities from Africa and India, that were conveyed north to Syria.

In Israel, at that time, King Solomon had created a navy with the timber supplied by Hiram, the king of Tyre, and it sailed from its base on the shore of the Red Sea in search of treasure. According to 1 Kings, 9:28: 'And they came to Ophir, and fetched from thence gold, four hundred and twenty talents, and brought it to King Solomon.' Then later, 1 Kings, 10:11: 'And the navy of Hiram, that brought gold from Ophir, bought in from Ophir great plenty of almug trees, and precious stones.' This led to the Queen of Sheba's celebrated visit to Solomon, when, swayed by his achievements and his personal magnetism she gave him 120 talents of gold; 'and he gave unto the Queen of Sheba all her desire, whatsoever she asked beside that which Solomon gave her of his royal bounty' (1 Kings 10:13). The royal house of Ethiopia claimed descent from this physical union. A romantic story of wealth, power and splendour, it evidently so intrigued James Cooper Dean that he commemorated it with Ophir Road and Ophir Gardens in Bournemouth.

And Ascham Road? What clue to his tastes and interests does this render? For an explanation we return with him to his adoptive Yorkshire. Roger Ascham (1515-68) was a humanist writer, classical scholar and courtier. Born of poor parents in the village of Kirby Wiske near Northallerton, 30 miles north of York, he was adopted by a rich patron, Sir Anthony Wingfield, who had him educated with his own sons and sent him in 1530 to St John's College, Cambridge, where he became an outstanding Greek scholar. His treatise on archery, published when he was 30, brought him praise and a pension from King Henry VIII. Subsequently tutor to the Princess Elizabeth for two years in 1548, an appointment from which he resigned owing to a quarrel with her steward, he next became secretary to the English ambassador at the court of the Emperor Charles V. Later, he was appointed secretary and tutor of Queen Elizabeth I.

His most important work was a treatise on education, *The Scholemaster*. James Cooper Dean, who to the end of his life possessed a sentimental regard for Yorkshire, had evidently learned of Ascham's remarkable achievements from humble beginnings when he lived and worked there. He pleased himself by commemorating them in Ascham Road. Thus, from these two unusual road names in Bournemouth something is revealed of his interests and character.

As his business interests grew, he moved into banking as a shareholder and director of the prosperous Wilts and Dorset Banking Company, whose Bournemouth branch was situated at 45-47 Old Christchurch Road, on land belonging to the Dean Park estate. He was appointed a director on 3 February 1909, his fellow directors being Captain Carr Stuart Glyn of Wimbourne, Colonel Charles Richard Luce, of Halcombe, Malmesbury, and the Earl of Radnor, Longford Castle, Salisbury. It is of interest that the bank, founded in 1835, had made a net profit in 1908 of £150,602 18s 9d from which it paid shareholders a dividend of 20 per cent tax-free. James Cooper Dean remained a director until its acquisition in 1914 by the rapidly expanding Lloyds Bank. He was then appointed a member of the Salisbury local committee set up by Lloyds to superintend the influx of business created by the amalgamation. He did not however rise to become a director of Lloyds Bank.

His main interest was always the development of the Bournemouth estates, and he appears to have chosen with care the builders to whom leases of building sites were sold, for the same names appear year after year — John Nethercoate, Kate

Holly, William Hoare, Frank Brewer, Davis & Lambert, George H. Rolls, Garnet Lambert, George & Harding and G. Shears & Son, among a number of others. In 1913, he named a newly-laid road in the Northwood estate, linking Talbot and Alma Roads, Stoke Wood Road, to commemorate his purchase of the Stoke Wood House estate, where from time to time he and cousin James Cooper organised their two-day shooting parties. Soberton Road, a turning off Queen's Park Drive South was given that name after Soberton parish, in which the Stoke Wood estate was partially situated.

He had been appointed a Governor of the Royal Victoria Hospital in 1909, so his association with it remained close. When in 1913 the hospital needed more land upon which to build an extension, as the owner of the adjoining land all eyes turned to him. He made the required site available for a peppercorn rent of five shillings a year, in an agreement signed on 25 March 1913. In those days of voluntary hospitals, he also helped financially the Royal Boscombe and West Hants Hospital, of which he was a trustee. Building in the Dean Estates and throughout Bournemouth slowed to a standstill during the First World War, but began to gather pace again in 1918, John Nethercoate leading the way with the construction of 34 to 44 Iddesleigh Road.

James Cooper Dean had for a lifetime played a major part in shaping the large areas of the town which he owned. In that period of its dramatic growth he had frequently shown by deeds how much he loved England's newest holiday resort. In 1919, in his 79th year, he looked, perhaps for the last time, to see what land he could still cede to the municipality for the permanent benefit of local people. Most obvious choice was the beautiful open expanse of grassy cliff-top, known as the West Cliff, divided by the sculptured pine-boardered chines above the sea, from Alum Chine to Westhill Road. The Bournemouth Corporation of the day had long been hopeful of acquiring it because, augmenting the land making up the West Overcliff Drive upon which he had already granted them leases on nominal terms in 1901 and 1902, their control of such a splendid local asset would be absolute, ruling out undesirable development projects by anyone for all time.

Negotiations between him and the Corporation were

straightforward, concluding with an agreement dated 10 December 1919 granting a 999-years-lease at £1,000 yearly, reducible to a nominal £236 6s a year provided the land conveyed was kept as an open space for public use. This being a book of record, it is of interest to note the land involved. It included: the triangular piece at the junction of Durley and Commercial Roads: two triangular pieces at the junction of Durley and West Cliff Roads: Durley Chine and Middle Chine: the eastern side of Alum Chine to the boundary of Middle Chine: land between the eastern and western boundaries of the Middle Chine and Durley Chine: the strips of land lying along the inner side of the Overcliff Drive and the piece of land 30 feet wide forming a pathway from the Durley Chine side of the Overcliff Drive to the Middle Chine side of it: the West Cliff frontage from Durley Chine to the Highcliffe Hotel: the strips of land on the north side of the land known as Durley Heath and abutting the West Cliff Road: and the Argyle Gardens — 'for public gardens for the use and benefit of the Lessees and Residents in the settled lands and for the inhabitants...'

Finally, an important clause in the agreement resolved the contentious issue of the extension of the Undercliff Drive, now Promenade, from the eastern boundary of the Dean West Cliff Estate to Alum Chine, which William Clapcott Dean had resolutely opposed. In 1919, James Edward Cooper Dean saw no point in opposing the extension any longer, for much of the Drive elsewhere had already been completed, leaving an extensive gap opposite the West Cliff estate.

The first part, Meyrick Road to Bournemouth Pier, had been opened in November 1907; the second, from the pier to the Cooper Dean West Cliff estate boundary, in January 1911; then from Alum Chine to the county boundary in 1912 and the section east of the pier in June, 1914. So, in this new agreement of 1919, James Cooper Dean consented that 'the Council shall be at liberty to continue the present Undercliff Promenade on the western side of Bournemouth pier... to Alum Chine...' The 1914-18 War delayed it, and not until October 1928 was the Council able to authorise the expenditure of £38,500 on the work, which was finished in 1930 and opened by Ellen Cooper Dean. It was a windy day and she held on tightly to her hat to prevent it being blown out to sea.

*James Cooper Dean in the grounds of Littledown House with his pet
terrier in 1920, shortly before his death at the age of 81. A master
builder by trade, he influenced the town development considerably
and gave land generously for schools, churches and public
recreation. His son Joseph inherited the family fortune.*

James Cooper Dean expected by the spirit and letter of this
agreement to have barred for all time developments in this
beautiful area of the town, by the Council, or anyone. It was
his final act of public generosity.

Henceforward, he spent his time at Littledown on the farms
and lands he loved, with friends and fellow shooting enthu-
siasts. Alice and Ellen still had rooms there and often drove
over to stay, while his chauffeur drove him along the country
roads to Stoke Wood House from time to time. Doubtless, he
regretted that neither of his daughters had ever married and
borne sons to perpetuate the name of Cooper Dean, especially
so since the children of Joseph, his only son, were also girls. It
was a sad step along the road to the extinction of the family.

161

Although Joseph remained estranged from his father, his two daughters, Ellen especially, were great friends with their grandfather. As a girl, Ellen used nearly every day to walk over to Littledown by the winding path over the open field from Pokesdown. 'I was terribly fond of Grandpa and one of my earliest recollections is of driving with him in the carriage-and-pair to his office in Hinton Road twice a week,' she told a friend. 'I used to be dolled up with bonnet and feathers — I adore feathers and always have done — and used to drive with the old man down to the office.'

While James Cooper Dean conferred with his land agent Mr Creeke, Ellen was taken for a drive through Bournemouth. 'The coachman was told to drive me along the West Cliff. We used to go through the Square, and there were only a few shops there then, in 1910. I thought it was all lovely — it was all beautifully open. There weren't many houses either.' Ellen also used to enjoy playing as a child on the Littledown farm with the farm workers' children who lived in the ancient thatched cottages on the estate.

'Grandfather took an enormous interest in the farm,' she remembered. 'He had two black-and-white St. Bernard dogs which went everywhere with him. He also had a black horse called Bendigo.' She thought of her childhood at Littledown as a lovely life, full of enjoyment despite her mother's early death, and remembered with pleasure a big natural lake upon which when it froze in winter she used to skate with her grandfather.

James Cooper Dean retained his health and strength right up to the day of his sudden death at Littledown on 16 August 1921. A jovial, likeable man, who had inherited these large areas of Bournemouth unexpectedly, he was prominently linked with its history for nearly 35 years, especially through his benevolence and his altruism in the field of public welfare.

Speculation as to the future of the estates ran high in the town.

CHAPTER 11

Land Sales

IN JAMES COOPER DEAN'S own words the will was written — 'my silver prize tea service, my silver cup presented to me by my sporting friends, the little clock in the billiard room, the gift to me of my mother, my piano and my pair of chestnut horses, harness and landau'. Cherished possessions, he left them to his daughters in a will made seven years before he died and, evidently satisfied with it, made no changes except for two codicils bequeathing funds that had accumulated.

The Dean Estates in Bournemouth, including Littledown, and the income from them, were entailed to Joseph Cooper Dean, who resided with his wife and daughters at Pokesdown Old Vicarage. But his own property James Cooper Dean chose to leave to those dearest to him, his daughters.

Father and son had remained estranged over the years and as a result Joseph inherited from his father three acres from the Iford estate, a meadow called Throop Meade at Muccleshill, a small property in Christchurch and 'the silver plate, plated articles, furniture, pictures ... my prize clock in the dining-room and the billiard table and fittings'. Bequeathed to him also were 'my gold watch and chain and my Napier motor car...'

James Cooper Dean gave his paternal love and generosity mainly to his daughters, Alice and Ellen. To them he also bequeathed the furniture in their bedrooms at Littledown, furniture and pictures in the drawing room and his most precious possessions. Joseph would need to do much re-furnishing of Littledown when he moved in. James Cooper Dean also left to his daughters as tenants in common the Iford estate of nearly 400 acres (except for the three acres left to Joseph); land and

***Edith Bethia (left), wife of Joseph Cooper Dean, with sister-in-law
Nell, both attired in formal Edwardian style, in a surprise
photograph taken on the shaded veranda of their home, Pokesdown
Old Vicarage.***

cottages at Great Dean, the Manor House, Porchester, proper-
ties at Holdenhurst which he had purchased in 1911 from
Lord Malmesbury and the 353-acre Bushy Down Farm,
Meonstoke, with its income of £250 a year.

Nor was this all of his intention to ensure the greatest possible security for them. They shared with their cousin, James
Cooper, a total of £15,350 in gilt-edged stock, shares in Lloyds
Bank and the capital sum of £12,000 secured by mortgages
that he had granted to various people. To James Cooper he left
in addition the West End estate at Hambledon adjoining his
daughters' Stoke Wood House, Droxford, together with more

164

land at Meonstoke, well stocked with game. He did not, however, forget Joseph's wife, Edith Bethia, who was his own blood relation, and for whom he had a special affection. He bequeathed her the Manor Farm House, Holdenhurst, for life, but upon her death it was to go to his daughters, not to Joseph.

Various other prized possessions he bequeathed to his cousin James, including the furniture from his bedroom at Littledown, as well as 'my prize field glasses, my gun and mahogany gun case and accessories, all the pictures, furniture and effects in my bedroom. And also all my personal property and effects at my West End estate hereafter devised to him, and my smaller motor car ...' A farm known as Wilson's Farm, at Sutton-on-the-Forest, near York, that he had acquired when in business there, he also left to Alice, Ellen and James Cooper in equal shares. James received in addition a block of shares in the West Hants Water Company. Other household effects of whatever nature in Littledown House not given to Joseph were to be divided equally between Alice and Ellen.

James Cooper Dean did not forget his household servants and farm workers. To Elizabeth Fisher, his housekeeper, Mary Ann Vivian, his cook, George Bennett, his groom, William Vatter, his gamekeeper, to James Gurd, Henry Vivian, George King and Frank Read, he left legacies of £50 each; to Annie Tuck and George Vine, whose duties were also not recorded, £50 each. But the main effect of his will was the showering of riches upon his already wealthy spinster-daughters, Alice and Ellen.

After his father's funeral and burial in the family grave, in Holdenhurst churchyard, Joseph moved from Pokesdown Old Vicarage to the grandeur of Littledown House with his wife Bethia, and his daughters Ellen, aged 22 and Edith, 19. Of medium height and stocky build, he was a very reserved, sometimes even diffident man, but forthright when pressed and given to occasional outbursts of temper. Ellen once remarked in a jocular way that at times he seemed frightened of his own shadow.

Joseph's schooling ended in his early teens, because he was not interested in it. His father decided his future would be more secure if he were to learn building and carpentering. This Joseph had done for two or three years, but relations between father and son were far from cordial. Joseph earned his living as best he could until he obtained regular work as a maintenance hand at the Belle Vue Gardens, Manchester, where a circus used to perform.

He was still working in this curious occupation in 1887 when his father inherited the Dean Estates. Since they were entailed to him he decided to leave Manchester and move south to Southsea. He lived on an income of £400 a year from the Dean Estates, married his cousin, Bethia Cooper, and in time fathered his two daughters, Ellen and Edith — not to be confused with their aunts, Alice and Ellen. Later, he lived in father's property, Pokesdown Old Vicarage.

From maintenance hand to heir to the Cooper Dean estates — it was a bizarre and extravagant turn of fortune. How would he respond to it? Though nearer to us in time than his forbears, Joseph Cooper Dean is an insubstantial figure in comparison. But we know something of his favourite pastimes. He loved football, golf, racing, billiards and cricket. A year or two after inheriting Littledown he had cricket and football pitches laid in the meadows, then organised two Littledown teams, the married men and the bachelors, who played against each other and local teams. He himself played in the cricket team in the Bournemouth cricket league, with varying success. Attending matches at the Dean Park Cricket Ground, he saw to it that the club never wanted for equipment. The billiards table he inherited is now played on by the local Boys' Brigade in Holdenhurst village hall.

Although he fished occasionally, his main outdoor sport was golf, played at all the local clubs, the Merrick and Queen's, the Parkstone and the Ferndown, where he was often partnered by Ellen. Never more than an average player, he was not prepared to take the trouble to master the game, just as having inherited his father's Napier car, he gave up learning to drive after a few attempts, and engaged a chauffeur. Playing billiards or cards with like-minded friends in Bournemouth was his indoor interest — whist, or poker for moderately high stakes, while sustained by whisky or brandy. Wine he rarely drank, even at the dinner table at home, where, too restless to sit and converse with his daughters for more than the very shortest time, he quickly finished eating, fed his pet Pekingese then jumped up

Edith Cooper Dean, Joseph's youngest daughter, aged 9, her hair and dress adorned with flowers. Neither she nor her elder sister, Ellen, both heiresses to a great fortune, ever married and the family became extinct.

and left the room, leaving them alone.

It took Joseph a long time fully to accustom himself to the possession of much money, and perhaps, as a result, he failed to equip Ellen and Edith with an appropiate education. Both girls attended small private schools, Ellen, the elder, Grovely Manor School nearby. Later, when mother, Edith Bethia, became ill she stayed at home looking after her. Ellen lacked education, in the academic sense, although she was extremely intelligent and perceptive, with a remarkable memory.

Dark eyed, slim and of medium height, she was shy and diffident where Edith, her sister, was tall, dominating and extrovert. Edith went to a small private school for young ladies at Lytchett Maltravers, but by the time she was 15 decided that study was boring, and refused to attend henceforward. So Ellen and Edith, two girls whose fortune could easily have taken them to a London season, with dances and the exciting marriage prospects that made up the glittering world of debutantes in the 1920s, stayed quietly at home with a melancholy father, their invalid mother having died a few months after arriving in Littledown.

Their world became somewhat limited. Instead of many friends of both sexes, Ellen and Edith possessed a few only of their own and fewer still of the opposite sex. Those young men whom they did meet and invite home their father suspected of chasing the family money. His reception of them was unwelcoming so they stayed away. It was a strange situation for the two young ladies of Littledown.

However, great wealth had, through the Finance Act of 1919, become the quarry of government in the 1920s to pay for the devastating cost of the 1914-18 World War, and Parliament voted huge increases in death duties. James Edward Cooper Dean's settled estate of £436,000 had been caught in the net. A hitherto unheard of 26 per cent duty, amounting to about £113,000 had to be found. The problem, how best to raise it, landed on the desks of Mr Edward Davy, of Rawlins, Davy & Wells, the solicitors, and of the old-established estate agents Fox & Sons. They had taken over management of the sale of building plots on the Dean Estates from Creeke, Gifford & Oakley, who carried on for the time being as surveyors.

William Fox and Joseph's solicitors appear to have realised at once that a radical change of policy was needed. Building plots should henceforward be sold freehold for cash, instead of for meagre annual ground rents with 99-year leases. And there were other reasons. The land, farmed at a loss, was of great value for building. Secondly, post-war inflation had lowered the real income from ground rents, while management costs

Ellen Cooper Dean, aged 5, enjoys her wheelbarrow ride in the gardens at Littledown House. She was shy and reticent, where her younger sister Edith was forthright and dominating in character.

rose steadily. From 1863, date of the first lease, to 1922, a total of 1,300 had been signed with an average rent of about £10 a year, giving an annual gross income of some £13,000, from which tax and running expenses were deducted before the Cooper Deans had their share. It left them with much territory but comparatively limited ready cash when money for death duties was urgently needed.

Meetings between Joseph Cooper Dean, Alice and Ellen, his two sisters, John Fox and solicitor Edward Davy, who had taken over from Walter Rawlins, led to the decision that even though land on the estates had never at any time in the past been systematically sold freehold, it would have to be done. So, it was agreed that at suitable intervals the Northwood, Iford, part of Littledown, then the Longbarrow estates would be auctioned freehold.

The decision was a milestone in the history of both the development of Bournemouth and of the Dean Estates. Henceforward, the way would be opened in Bournemouth to an influx of a multitude of new residents owning their houses freehold, who would bring a more youthful character to the town.

The plans for the sales were doubtless those of William Fox, the firm, it is interesting to note, having been founded in 1868 by Anthony Stoddart Fox, 31 years before the opening of their first Bournemouth office at 36 Holdenhurst Road in 1889. William Fox, youngest son of the founder, had opened a branch at 44 Old Christchurch Road in 1904. But Joseph Cooper Dean liked to be kept in the picture. They met every Thursday with Edward Davy, and in his forthright good-humoured way Fox established a working relationship with Joseph, although the first time that Joseph strode into his office wearing a cloth cap and an old jacket he had asked him if he had come for a road-laying job. Joseph shook his head. 'I'm the new owner, Joe Cooper Dean,' he responded, nervously. It was Fox's turn to be embarrassed, but they shook hands and soon were on Christian name terms. Later, Joe had his revenge. When one of the new roads in the Queen's Park area of Littledown was to be named, he called it William Road, explaining that it was so called either after his own pet dog, a Peke named William, or after William Fox. People could take their choice. Joe Cooper Dean had an ironic sense of humour.

Development of the Eastwood estate, between Queen's Park South Drive and Richmond Park Road, had started in the early 1920s. Bethia Road there was so named in 1922, following the death of Joseph's wife, Edith Bethia, that year, after a long illness. Her death had shattered the family, for her good humour and kindness had kept them together. Family bonds, frail as they already were, became noticeably weakened as time went on. Thenceforward, Joseph always had her favourite flowers, pink carnations, on the dinner table.

A year later, in 1923, began the freehold sales. Creeke, Gifford and Oakley first surveyed the Northwood estate, laid out roads and numbered the building plots to be sold. Lying between Alma Road, Grafton Road, Iddlesleigh Road, Charminster Road and Wimborne Road it held some 325 plots ranging from 90 feet wide and 200 feet long, to as small as 50 feet by 130 feet.

Fox & Sons sold the land in two separate auctions, the first, of 124 plots on 24 and 25 January 1923 at the Havergal Hall, Post Office Road, Bournemouth; then 77 plots on 11 July 1923 and 93 plots on 29 January 1924 at the same hall. The sales were a success in so far as builders, prominent among whom was John Nethercoate, outbid each other in their efforts to secure these valuable plots on the fringes of the ever-expanding town. But the first object was not realised, for insufficient money had been raised to settle outstanding death duties and further sales had soon to be made. However, completion of Cooper-Dean building development elsewhere went ahead, including houses in Chine Crescent, and Durley Road; parts of Iddlesleigh and Soberton Roads, number 13 Beechey Road, built by George & Harding; five houses, numbers 387 to 407, in the upper reaches of Holdenhurst Road, another six, 28 to 34, in Methuen Road, 40 to 42 Littledown Road for the Bournemouth Steam Laundry in 1924, and in 1925 a second branch of Lloyds Bank in Lansdowne Crescent, both of these with previously arranged 99-years-leases.

The auctioning of plots on the Iford and Littledown estates between King's and Queen's Parks began. James Edward Cooper Dean had, of course, bought Iford with the object of keeping new house-building away from his adjoining Littledown estate, but this was no longer feasible. Iford could not remain an island of green in the built-up residential areas of Boscombe, Pokesdown and Southbourne. Sheer economics demanded that Iford follow suit.

Alice and Ellen Cooper Dean, to whom it had been left by their father, undoubtedly needed the money from the impending sales because their farms at Stoke Wood, Droxford, were operating at a loss, while the upkeep of the estate was heavy. They did not forget their father's generosity towards the Bournemouth community however, and responded to appeals in an open-handed way. In 1928, they gave a substantial area of land at the corner of Swanmore Road and Hambledon Road to Bournemouth as a pleasure ground for local people. Now known, of course, as Swanmore Gardens, it is popular for tennis and bowls. Three years later in response to an appeal for help, the sisters gave a plot measuring 240 by 141 feet at the corner of Ropley and Coleman Roads, as a site for a new Congregational Church; then in 1933, a large site at the corner of Holdenhurst Avenue and Colemore Road for St. Saviour's Church of England. These largely forgotten gifts testify again to the traditional generosity of the Cooper Dean family towards the town.

Fox & Sons had sensibly divided the Iford estate into 15 separate sections, with auctions timed to occur at intervals over eleven years between 1923 and 1934 in order to maintain prices and not devalue the land. William Fox presided over the first auction in a marquee on the estate on 7 June 1923, when 81 plots between Corhampton, Christchurch and Southwick Roads averaging 130 by 40 feet were on offer. Builders bid enthusiastically, especially after the buffet lunch of roast beef or cold salmon and salad, with generous draughts of beer, provided *gratis*. The total receipts of this first sale more than recouped James Cooper Dean's original £20,100 purchase money for the entire Iford estate.

Henceforward, the auctions and sales by private treaty

Joseph Cooper, seen in this portrait by an unknown artist, married Elizabeth Dean, daughter of Richard Dean. His son, James Edward Cooper, inherited the estates from William Clapcott Dean, who never married. (Photo: MORRIS BENJAMIN)

continued over the years at intervals timed to enable builders to develop the land they had acquired. The second, 96 plots between Harewood Avenue, Hambledon Road, the railway, Southwick, Corhampton and Christchurch Roads, with plots once more averaging 40 by 100 feet, took place on 16 September 1924. Receipts again exceeded the original purchase money of the whole estate, as did each sale subsequently. William Fox held two more in September 1927, another in September 1929, none in 1930 (presumably so that builders could catch up) but one each during the next four years. The last one, containing 102 plots, bounded by Holdenhurst Avenue, Castle Lane, Christchurch Road and Colemore Road occurred on 12 June 1934. Altogether on the Iford estate, in the Pokesdown Hill area, some 1,800 plots had been sold by Alice and Ellen, either by private treaty or auction.

Happy memories of their home and its surroundings they commemorated in their choice of the names of the Iford-Pokesdown roads, taken from hamlets and villages around Stoke Wood: these included Cheriton, Colemore, Corhampton, Denmead, Droxford, Durrington, Exton, Hambledon, Hursley, Meon, Ovington, Petersfield, Ropley Southwick, Swanmore, Waltham and Warnford. Stoke Wood was commemorated in the Northwood estate, the village of Soberton in the Queen's Park district and the name Cooper Dean, as an extension of Queen's Park Avenue, in Cooper Dean Drive.

Joseph Cooper Dean, on the other hand, showed his admiration for royalty and his strong attachment to Yorkshire. To commemorate the wedding of Princess Mary (the Princess Royal) and the Viscount Lascelles (later Earl of Harewood) in 1922, he decided that the boundary road between Littledown and King's Park should be named Harewood Avenue, and the small road parallel to it running into Christchurch Road, Lascelles Road. The remaining boundaries of the new development were named Littledown Drive, Littledown Avenue and Thistlebarrow Road. Between them ran Leeson Road, William Road, Gainsborough Road and Glencoe Road.

William Fox was in due course ready for the Littledown sales. The first auction, 62 plots ranging from 40 to 60 feet frontage, depth up to 178 feet, in the western end of the area between Holdenhurst Road, King's Park Drive, Littledown

Avenue and Thistlebarrow Road, was held on 27 April 1926. Would-be builders crowded into the marquee, studying plans with marked and numbered plots. By early afternoon all had been sold at an average price, incredible today, of £150 an acre. The second sale, 42 building plots between the same two main roads, took place two months later on 1 July, all of them again being quickly sold by auction or private treaty.

Four years later, in 1930, the long association between the Dean family and the land agents and surveyors Creeke, Gifford & Oakley, ended when the firm ceased business. Fox & Sons, who already acted as the family's estate agents, were in September of that year appointed surveyors too, the firm's senior surveyor, Aubrey Goadsby, moving into its Hinton Chambers office, where he worked for the next 40 years.

At this time in the 1920s, central Bournemouth faced an onslaught by property developers that destroyed much of its Victorian architectural heritage. Some of the new buildings were acceptable, other simply shoddy and unworthy of their environment. The first of the Westover Road villas had been well-converted for shops and business use before the First World War, a process set back in the 1930s with the erection of what was then called a super-cinema. The Bath Road, with its large villas in spacious gardens, inevitably succumbed to commercialisation in the 1930s when the municipality began a much-needed road-widening scheme. In the 1970s many Dean Estates properties were demolished to make way for Wessex Way, running from Richmond Hill to the borough boundary. But many of the old villas have survived in the Dean Park area, for example in Dean Park Road, and still many more on the West Cliff, which has kept something of its original character, despite the replacement of the old unwanted houses by blocks of flats.

After a pause of six years in marketing the Littledown plots, to enable builders to develop them and those at Iford, approximately another 80 between Holdenhurst and Leeson Roads, facing the Queen's Park golf course, were sold on 12 May 1932, to be followed a year later on 20 July 1933, by the sale of 47 plots on either side of William Road. Three years later, on 11 June 1936, came the final sale of 51 plots on either side of Gainsborough Road, and between Littledown Avenue and

Harewood Avenue, making a total of 282 altogether. It had been a profitable undertaking both for the Cooper Dean Estates and for Bournemouth.

Much satisfaction was expressed between Joseph Cooper Dean, Alice and Ellen, William Fox and local builders, following what they saw as a timely release of this inferior agricultural land for building.

The last of the Cooper Dean land sales, in the Longbarrow estate between Castle Lane West, Woodbury Avenue and Throop Road, including Hastings and Barrow Roads and Crantock Grove, took place on 19 May 1936. Of the 113 building plots there, 25 had been sold by private treaty before the auction, when the remainder found ready bidders. Between that date and 11 October 1938 the remaining 314 plots were sold, for the housebuilding boom continued despite the prevailing political uncertainty, as Hitler's Nazi armies threatened the peace of Europe.

Joseph Cooper Dean, satisfied at the success of the auctions, remembered the generosity of his forbears. He gave a large site on the corner of Castle Lane West and Woodbury Avenue for the Eventide Homes for retired and elderly people; another near Throop Road for the Holdenhurst Community Centre in 1933 and in 1937 a site for the Retired Nurses' National Home in Riverside Avenue.

Meanwhile, his only worry was about the marriage prospects of his two daughters. He was desperately anxious that they should marry and have children to carry on the line. What hopes were there of marriage for these two rich young ladies?

CHAPTER 12

Destiny Frowns

GREAT HOPES WERE held in the 1920s that one if not both of Joseph Cooper Dean's attractive daughters would marry and have children to bear the family name, inherit its wealth and oversee the management of its housing estates in Bournemouth. But, after 200 years, destiny, as we shall see, was to play an adverse hand in these castles in the air.

The older generation — Joseph, his two sisters, Alice and Ellen, of Stoke Wood House, Droxford, and his cousin James Cooper, of West End House, Hambledon — agreed that Edith, the younger daughter, would be sure to marry and have a family. Tall, with a good figure, extrovert, attractive to men and attracted by them, she seemed destined for an early, fruitful marriage.

About her elder sister Ellen's marriage prospects the family were a bit less certain. Very pretty, with dark brown eyes and a deep contralto voice that contrasted with a shy, reticent manner, but sustained her strongly independent ways, she was gentle and charming behind her defensive façade. Her aunts agreed that only a sympathetic and clever man of whose devotion she was certain would be able to win her heart. Such men being somewhat rare, Ellen seemed a little less likely than Edith to ensure the family's future.

The sisters' lives had already in their twenties taken different ways. Ellen looked after the domestic routine at Littledown, managing the house, the servants and the cook. Edith helped her father to run the Littledown and Holdenhurst farms, and it was thought likely that she would find a husband from among the young land-owning farmers whom she met at the local markets and agricultural shows.

Then came a setback that set all these hopes at nought. Aged 24, Edith became ill and had to undergo a gynaecological operation. When she had fully recovered she was told that she would never be able to bear children.

A verdict from which there could be no appeal, it was also a deep emotional shock. Though younger by three years than Ellen, she had come to see herself as the one upon whom the family's future depended, in imagination casting herself in the role of a mother-figure from whose marriage would be borne a son or sons to perpetuate the family name, and inherit its wealth. She had embraced the idea, in a sense committed herself to it, having no doubt that she would be able to find the right man. The prospect had cast a rosy glow over the future.

But now, with these expectations at an end, everything had changed. In a rational way, she accepted the situation once she had overcome her initial distress, without apparently looking over her shoulder at what might have been. About one thing she made up her mind: since she could not bear children she would never marry. That particular dream was over.

The event had its effects. Her personality changed, she became harder, aggressive. Ellen's show of sympathy for her she rebuffed, perhaps jealously aware that in a sense she herself had become a back number, for the family's hopes of an heir now dwelt upon Ellen; she herself had failed them. As for the family, the prospect of their dynasty coming to an end after 250 years was felt to be a tragedy.

Joseph, her father, was deeply sorry for her. He tried to help in the only way he understood, that is materially. He bought her a new Rolls-Royce, gave her a lavish supply of money and sent her off for a tour of the cities and playgrounds of France and Italy for several weeks — not with Ellen, who stayed at home, but alone except for a chauffeur-courier engaged a few days before through an agency. What sort of holiday it was we can only guess; beautiful scenery hardly helps someone alone with a sense of sorrow.

Ellen, meantime, was in an unenviable situation, the family's expectations centred upon her, but she was determined to be true to her own convictions. For her, marriage was by no means a priority. Should she meet and like a suitable man, well and good, otherwise — she shrugged her slim shoulders — it

178

didn't matter at all. She was unimpressed by the family's recent performance and although she loved her own immediate relations she felt that an unlucky streak dogged their lives, including her own, leading to unhappiness. 'We're an extraordinary, eccentric bunch,' she once said to a friend. 'I think we are due to come to an end, and I'm not sorry.' It was a harshly realistic judgement from a gentle person.

Joseph's attitude to her marrying was somewhat inconsistent, for while professing a wish for it he was often unwelcoming towards the few men friends that she had. One relationship with a pleasant young man of whom she believed she might grow fond came to nought for this reason. William Jones, of Lloyds Bank in Bournemouth, used to cash her cheques. They chatted frequently across the counter, for in this unromantic atmosphere Ellen shed her shyness. They went dancing, and one Sunday she invited him to Littledown for tea. Her father strode into the room, and she introduced them. Joseph gave the young man a searching look, shook hands then left the room and did not return. That evening he told Ellen: 'You can't marry him. I won't have it. That's an end to it!' Whether or not Ellen had ever thought of him as a possible husband we do not know, but in contrast to her usual independent ways, she accepted her father's disapproval of the relationship and ended it.

Not long afterwards, in the early 1920s, she began an affair with a handsome young RAF officer, Flight Lieutenant Alistair —???—, of whom she had become genuinely fond. They had met by chance in the Paddington to Bournemouth train, conversed to while away the time and found themselves mutually attracted. Though still somewhat shy, Ellen was always attractive, beautifully dressed to the last detail of hats, gloves, and shoes, her quiet personality offset by the appeal of her dark brown eyes and deep voice. He was stationed near Bournemouth, so they met frequently, usually for dinner and dancing — the foxtrot, and the tango. Ellen invited him up to Littledown, where Joseph, appreciating him as a suitable husband for her, made much of him.

The future looked promising, and Ellen was happy. Then quite suddenly their romance was brought to an untimely end. At two or three days' notice Alistair was posted with his squadron to the Far East. They had time only for one farewell meeting, persuading themselves it would not be for long, promising to write often. Letters sped between them, then for three weeks there was silence. At last, came a letter to her from a fellow officer. He sent the news that Alistair had been killed in a flying crash.

For Ellen, this bleak and sudden end to the life of the only man for whom she had ever cared was a tragedy. She found consolation in reading poetry, in particular a poem by the minor poet Gerald Gould, suggesting that life recurs in another dimension after bodily death. Having copied it out she put it among her private papers, where it was found after her own death. The poem that echoed Ellen's feelings is worth reading for its insight into her character and sensibility:

If we met no more,
Having parted,
Would things be as before
For the broken-hearted?
Would the rain fall?
Would the sun shine?
Would anything at all
Be yours or mine?

If death meant dying,
If love could pass,
Think you, would the birds
have wings for flying?
Would flowers be born amid
the grass?

Surely all beautiful things
Shall always be ours —
Remember the beating of wings
And the shining of flowers.

Henceforward, she gave up the hope and even the wish for any permanent relationship likely to lead to marriage. For her, like her sister Edith, it became a thing of the past. She had a variety of men friends, none of whom she took seriously and all of whom she kept more or less at arm's length. Still fond of ballroom dancing, when it was much in vogue in the early

1930s, she used to dance regularly at the local hotels, but mainly with professionals, who received a fee for their services. It was a diversion that helped to reconcile her to the loss of Alistair without risk of emotional or physical entanglements. 'There's no danger in it,' she used to say. A woman friend, Jay Wilson, also dance-mad, used to accompany her.

At the same time, Ellen continued to keep house at Little-down for her father, Edith having now become his deputy in the management of the farms, which she enjoyed and to which she completely devoted herself, while making sure that Ellen had no part in it. 'It would be impossible,' she used to say, 'Ellen's afraid of cows!' This *fait accompli*, backed by their father, Ellen had no other course but to accept.

Tensions between them, arising out of home circumstances no less than their incompatible characters, worsened to the point where life for the more sensitive Ellen in lonely, inhar-monious Littledown became too difficult. After housekeeping there for the ten years since her mother's death — chasing the reluctant housemaids responsible for keeping the 16-roomed house spick and span, ensuring that the cook produced what was required to please her father, providing a constant supply of fresh vegetables, meat and dairy produce from the farms — she felt at the age of 33 that it was time that she had a life of her own. But where could she go?

She thought of a plan. To her friend Jay Wilson she pro-posed that they should buy a house and live there together, and not surprisingly the idea appealed to Jay. Since childhood she had been an orphan, and was then living with relatives. But how would they pay for the proposed house? Jay had enough money of her own to live on, plus a little more, but Ellen, strange as it may seem, had only a small allowance from her father and a little money in the bank. Nor, she thought was her father likely to finance a scheme that would lose him a house-keeper, and of which he disapproved. The bank, in those days of economic depression, would be unlikely to grant them a loan; and their chances with a building society seemed scarcely better, for in the early 1930s the societies were less numerous, less supplied with scarce money and so more selective about to whom they granted a mortgage.

In the end, she turned to her father, and Joseph agreed to

lend her the money through an interest-free mortgage. A few days later they contracted to buy a small house at nearby Milford-on-Sea. Except for the road, a low wall and the sands, nothing lay between them and the sea, which, on the summer's day when they decided to buy, was invitingly calm, blue and sparkling. It seemed idyllic with the ocean-going liners sailing by, and a month later they moved in, although on Ellen's part not without some heartache at leaving Littledown. She still loved its space and beauty, its superb panorama, the deer roaming the park, the teeming wildlife — the pheasants, partridges, woodcock, the play of hares in the fields and, most of all, on early summer nights, the nightingales that sang in the clump of trees near her bedroom window. So she was sad to go and sadder still that family discord had forced her to do so. But she settled down happily with Jay, in their new home. For the first time in her life she knew the joy of total freedom, of being able to come and go as she pleased and being able to entertain her own friends, instead of being tied to a regime that was not hers.

Summer in that little house by the sea seemed to Ellen like a long holiday, but the winters were less appealing. Gales buffeted the walls and windows, while the waves crashed ever nearer on the beach, trying furiously, it seemed, to engulf them, but they persuaded themselves not to be nervous. Then one February night, their third year, gales lashed the house as never before, while the sound of the waves grew even louder, nearly subduing the sound of music to which they were listening.

Suddenly, a huge wave struck the south-facing French windows with a mighty crash, burst them open and flooded waist high with foaming sea water the little sitting-room where they sat. They forced their way through, relieved to reach the staircase and safety. The sea had done its worst, there were no more angry waves and the night grew quieter. But for Ellen and Jay it was enough. Joseph having discharged the mortgage for them, they sold the house several weeks later and bought another in New Milton. At Ellen's wish they named it Little Dene, in memory of her old home.

Meanwhile, Edith had invited an old friend and former nurse, Cecily Appleby, called 'Apple', to stay with her at Littledown to take over Ellen's former housekeeping job and look after her father, while she managed the farms, for Joseph had grown too old to do it. But to give Edith a day off, Ellen, who was fond of cycling, rode the 16 miles there and back to Littledown every Friday. She liked to see her father every week.

Joseph Cooper Dean was 72 in 1938 and the question of providing for his daughters in the future began to worry him. He bitterly regretted having to accept the fact that the family had run its course, and that sooner or later the day would come when there would be no more Cooper Deans in Bournemouth.

He therefore decided to make new arrangements, and instructed his solicitors, Rawlins, Davy & Wells, to disentail the Dean Estates entirely, so that he would be free to do as he wished. This having been done, he made over the whole of the West Cliff estate, the remainder of the Northwood and Eastwood estates, as well as the Manor Farm, Holdenhurst, all together worth a vast sum, jointly to Ellen and Edith. A little later, he purchased Holdenhurst Farm from his sisters and transferred this also to his daughters.

It was joyful news for them. For the first time they had incomes of their own, and a share in the family estates. But Joseph Cooper Dean did not fully achieve what he set out to do, namely, avoid the severe death duties to which the Estates were to be subjected, for he died shortly before the statutory period.

Barely 12 months later the Second World War started, and from the outset the two sisters played their part in the national effort. Edith became a V.A.D. nurse; Ellen and her friend Jay joined the WVS. Ellen bought, equipped and stocked with supplies at her own expense a mobile canteen in which, daily from early morning to dusk, for six, sometimes seven days a week, she and Jay visited the numerous military units in the New Forest area selling — and often giving — cigarettes, chocolate, cups of coffee and tea to soldiers and airmen. Day after day it was demanding work, for this tranquil coastal area had become, as a D-day invasion base the target of repeated enemy air raids.

Altogether, in Bournemouth and its surroundings, the Luftwaffe dropped a total of 2,271 bombs, starting on 3 July 1940 with the destruction in Cellar Farm Road, Southbourne, of one house and severe damage to 19 others. A little later, the House of Bethany's orphanage wing was blown apart, fortunately while the orphans were evacuated. Next, Luftwaffe bombers dropped six land mines by parachute, damaging over 2,300 houses in Westbourne, killing 53 people, wounding many more. A bomb struck Skerrymore, one-time home of Robert Louis Stevenson, demolishing the house and killing

The Methodist Punchion Church on Richmond Hill was bombed in an enemy air raid in May, 1943. The same bomb destroyed part of the popular Central Hotel, believed to have been the main target.

soldiers billeted there. Christ Church, in Alumhurst Road suffered extensive damage, the school in Alma Road was devastated, while several houses there were razed, again with a number of people killed.

As Ellen soon learned, no one knew where and when the enemy attacks would come. In a heavy raid on 23 May 1943 high explosive and incendiary bombs crashed down in 10 different districts. The Central Hotel on Richmond Hill and the Metropole at the corner of Christchurch and Holdenhurst Roads were both demolished. (An observant air raid warden reported soon afterwards that he spotted a swarm of rats scuttling up Holdenhurst Road.) Another bomb blew up Beale's Store, igniting gas from the main which burnt the rubble to ashes. Altogether, 219 people were killed and hundreds injured, 75 houses or business premises were totally destroyed, another 3,481 badly damaged.

Servicemen in the camps outside the town knew they could depend upon Ellen's arrival with a canteen of goodies and, under the nickname of 'Kay' she became known for her reliability under all conditions. The letter of appreciation she received from the WVS at the end of the war testifies to her courage and tenacity. 'Kay Dear — What can I say and how can I express what I feel about you and your work during these past more than five years,' wrote Mary Gilliat Naylor, the WVS chief for the region, in a letter dated 14 August 1945.

You leave with the satisfaction above all of many jobs oh! so well done, and of having earned a reputation unsurpassed by any one in the Borough of making a success of everything that you do. You have created an atmosphere of "all's well" wherever you've been, as even Miss Leigh Spencer in far off 'County' realised.

What you have meant to a very over-burdened B.O. (Borough Officer) in the emergency years you will probably never quite realise, for I just can't begin to express it. You have been the backbone and foundation of so many vital aspects of our responsibilities . . . I shall never forget as will none of those who have come in contact with you, from the evacuees to the Forces, and the traders to the powers-that-be . . . your complete selflessness and untiring (on the surface) efforts on all their behalfs.

WVS has stood for a great deal all over the County and not

least of all here, and I who am so very proud to be a member of it am most deeply and sincerely grateful to you who have played such a very great part in it. May you reap the reward you deserve and may we have very many happier times together when Jay is well . . . A last big Thank You, from Yours truly appreciative Mary Gilliat Naylor.

In this war work Ellen Cooper Dean discovered her true potential. She was determined, capable, friendly, successful and generous. Above all, she created a happy atmosphere, and she never gave up.

During the immediate post-war years Ellen and her friend Jay Wilson lived quietly together in their home Little Dene, New Milton. Quietly, because neither of them was in good health. Two cheerful, undaunted invalids, they moved later into their own suite on the top floor of Bournemouth's Carlton Hotel, where Ellen's two elderly aunts, Alice and Ellen, were then living, having sold their much-loved Stoke Wood House with its accompanying land at Droxford to Mr Tom Parker, a local farmer and sportsman.

Edith, meanwhile, continued living at Littledown with her friend Cecily Appleby, managing the farms while 'Apple' looked after her father, Joseph, who by this time needed constant care. In 1946, he gave a valuable piece of land as a site for the War Memorial Homes, true to the last to the family tradition of philanthropy. In 1950, aged 84, he had lost his sight and it was clear would not live for long. His death would lead to the eventual extinction of the family and to the sale of the Littledown estate. It would affect the future shape of Bournemouth more than anything else.

CHAPTER 13

The Big Sale

ELLEN COOPER DEAN and her sister Edith had together become proprietors and landlords of about a quarter of the residential and business areas of Bournemouth by 1950. The Dean Estates had increased hugely in value but ironically, while the family had never been so rich it was on the brink of extinction. Ellen and Edith would be the last ever to bear the name of Cooper Dean.

Joseph Cooper Dean had made his will in December 1949, six months before he died on 2 July 1950. To Ellen and Edith he left the Dean Estates, including Littledown, as well as investments amounting to £342,712 to be divided equally between them. Already, in 1938, it will be remembered, he had made over to them a major part of the Estates, thus avoiding heavy death duties while at the same time providing for his daughters.

Joseph also left Edith, his favourite, all his furniture, china, pictures, carpets and other contents of Littledown House, as well as his motor cars and the stock of farm implements and animals. It was his last show of preference for his younger daughter, this denial to Ellen of any share in the things associated with her youth in the family home, and it wounded her. He also left £100 to Ellen's friend Jay Wilson, and to Edith's companion 'Apple', who had nursed him during his illness, £500. Apart from legacies for the farm and domestic staff varying from £100 to £10, he also gave £100 each to four relations living in Yorkshire.

The 1950s were times of last farewells for the Cooper Deans. A few months after the death of Joseph, his sister Alice Elizabeth died, leaving £129,086 to their surviving sister, Ellen

187

Ann. She also bequeathed £1,000 each to her favourite charities — Holdenhurst Elderly Nurses' Homes, the Eventide Homes in Bournemouth, and £100 each to Dr Barnado's Homes, John Groom's Cripplage, the Royal National Mission to Deep Sea Fishermen, St Dunstan's and the Salvation Army, all of which she had helped in the past.

Ellen Ann Cooper Dean, the surviving sister, lived alone in her Carlton Hotel suite for another six years before she died in her eighties in 1957. She left a substantial sum of money to be divided between her two nieces, Ellen and Edith, and again a range of legacies to a long list of charities. To Ellen, of whom she was fond, she also left a diamond brooch and her large but very old-fashioned wardrobe, with which Ellen was at her wits' end to know what to do.

What manner of lives were the two Cooper Dean sisters then living? Edith happily and efficiently ran Littledown farm and travelled occasionally in Europe with her friend 'Apple'. In good health, she was expected by her medical advisers to live on to a ripe old age.

Ellen's life was less agreeable. She and her friend Jay Wilson resided in a suite in Bournemouth's luxurious Carlton Hotel, their every want provided for, but it was a sad and lonely existence, for by the early 1950s Jay had become a permanent invalid. Ellen, spending all her time helping to nurse her, was also in poor health. Only a few friends came to see them. Ellen sold the house, Little Dene, at New Milton, which they realised they would never occupy again, after having given away all the furniture. Despite her great wealth, this confined regime was the measure of Ellen's life. It ended in 1966 when Jay died, aged 59. She bequeathed £1,000 to the hotel staff and the rest of her small fortune to Ellen.

Aged 67, Ellen faced a bleak future. Shy and introverted, depressed at the loss of her friend and close companion over 30 years, she had reached a melancholy cross-roads in her life, with few friends and few absorbing interests. The Estates were well looked after by lawyers and agents. But she liked to help people in need, which she did frequently and in secret, finding it gave her life some meaning. As trustees of the Dean Estates, she and Edith also made occasional gifts of land to educational or religious bodies, the most recent being the site in 1969 for

188

St Barnabas Church, Mount Pleasant Drive, near Cooper Dean Drive.

She read the newspapers avidly, enjoyed novels and light music, but did not socialise, play bridge or other card games and was not inclined to take part in church life. Nor had she associations with the farming community, which gave so much pleasure and interest to her sister. Her main leisure interest was racing. Having placed modest bets on runners that took her fancy, she watched the events on television.

But she was alone at the Carlton when Jay was admitted to hospital. With sisterly concern, even before Jay died, Edith insisted that she return to live in her old rooms at Littledown, and this Ellen did, for the first time for 30 years. It was a thoughtful act, but having regard to the lifelong incompatibility between the two sisters, some friction between them was inevitable. So, even back at Littledown, these were cheerless days for Ellen. She was no less isolated and her health had not improved.

Then, surprisingly, came a new relationship and with it a welcome change of lifestyle. Three years earlier, in 1963, an orthopaedic consultant had treated her for arthritis and recommended physiotherapy by Miss Sylvia Bowditch, who practised conveniently close in Westbourne. For three years she gave Ellen the prescribed treatment thrice weekly and they became close friends. They had somewhat similar backgrounds. Like Ellen, Sylvia Bowditch was descended from Dorsetshire farmers. They also shared an interest in racing, while Sylvia's straightforward, independent and forthright character was like a breath of fresh air to Ellen. On her part, Sylvia discovered beneath Ellen's shyness a sweet and gentle woman with an appealing sense of humour.

Their friendship was interrupted when Sylvia went briefly to live and work elsewhere. Three months' later, responding to Ellen's request for urgent physiotherapy, she drove to see her at Littledown and was dismayed to observe that her weight had fallen to about seven stone, far too little even for her modest build and height. Ellen's doctor recommended that a change of environment was necessary for her even to begin to get better. So Sylvia proposed in the following spring of 1967 that they should go on holiday together in Ireland, and to this Ellen happily agreed. 'I've never in my life been farther away from Bournemouth than the Isle of Wight or London,' she declared — a revealing confession that astonished Sylvia.

They flew to Ireland — incredibly, Ellen's first flight — hired a car in Dublin and drove north through country with which Sylvia was familiar, to Rosapenna, a pretty little town on the north coast of County Donegal, thence down the west coast to Limerick and back to Dublin. They visited the Irish national stud, the Leopardstown races and the Dreaper stables, home of the famous steeple-chaser Arkle, winner of the Cheltenham Gold Cup. Sylvia was a friend of Betty Dreaper (now Lady Thomson) and had stayed with her in the past.

Perhaps for the first time since her childhood Ellen found that she could enjoy herself. To visit the racing stables in Ireland and watch the sleek two-year-old thoroughbreds training re-awoke the attraction that racing had had for her since girlhood, but which the confined circumstances of her life had limited to watching on television. Sylvia had loved the sport since she was a girl and this shared interest strengthened the bonds of their friendship. After returning from Ireland they began to visit the races together regularly and talked of the possibility of Ellen owning a racehorse herself.

In 1968, they attended the racing season at Ascot and there, acting on impulse, Ellen bought an apartment. They moved in together, making it a base for their race-going while at the same time studying the performances of horses, trainers and jockeys — everything connected with flat racing — with care. Ellen placed bets, and generally won more than she lost, which added to the excitement. Later, they also travelled to the Italian lakes, to Switzerland and in the winter to Madeira.

It was an exciting new life for Ellen and she thrilled to it. But despite their lively social life she began to wish for a more spacious, quieter home than the Ascot apartment, with its unending noise of traffic. She began to look at country houses on the market, and in 1972 bought an attractive period house near Henley-on-Thames into which she and Sylvia moved. In peaceful countryside, it was still not far from Ascot and handy also for Newbury and Salisbury racecourses. Together, they were by now members of all three.

Between them a firm and close friendship had grown. Ellen recognised in Sylvia a staunch friend and confidant upon whose support she could always rely. Knowledge of it gave her renewed self-confidence. She no longer felt isolated, and made it clear that she wished their relationship to become permanent. As a physiotherapist, Sylvia had grown used to giving physical and emotional help to people who needed it. She had begun by helping Ellen similarly, and had grown to like her for herself. Now that they were friends and companions she enjoyed their interesting life together, just as she helped Ellen to enjoy herself. But she had always been free and independent, so she hesitated over the sacrifice of this it would mean, until that is, she began to comprehend how much Ellen would miss her. Then she agreed, and they lived under the same roof thenceforward.

Meanwhile, the idea of owning her own racehorses fascinated Ellen more and more. She knew her pleasure in the sport would double when her own horses were running. At the same time, however, thoughts of owning a farm of her own began to excite her, for though she had lived for some years on the Littledown farm she regretted that she had never had any part in the management of it. She had always longed to do so.

But to indulge herself so fully, to own racehorses and a farm, she would need a large sum, whereas as co-owner of the Cooper Dean Estates, she received just a half share of the income. In addition, she spent lavishly on 19th century Dutch and French paintings, on hats, dresses and shoes, usually three or four pairs of the most costly variety at a time, in the hope that one pair would prove comfortable. There was also her collection of beautiful and expensive handbags, to which she was continually adding, her contributions to charity and her help for private individuals, all of which she enjoyed.

In 1972, Rawlins, Davy & Wells, lawyers for the Dean

Overleaf:

Littledown House, built to the order of John Dean about 1798, is seen in this aerial photograph enclosed in its girdle of trees in the centre of over 100 acres of meadowland and pasture. It was acquired by Bournemouth Corporation in 1973, for occupation 11 years later, and subsequently sold to Chase Manhattan Bank at a handsome profit. (KITCHENHAM LIMITED)

Estates, inadvertently provided a solution. Pointing out with becoming tact that the sisters — Ellen, 73 and Edith 70 — lacked heirs and were well advanced in years, they suggested that it would be sensible, instead of holding on, to sell Littledown House and its 136 acres of parklands to Bournemouth Corporation, who were known to be interested in buying the land for housing development. Ellen and Edith would thus have money at their disposal to enjoy as they wished.

Both of the sisters saw the soundness of the proposal although Ellen had doubts and agreed reluctantly, after urging that the area north of the house should be kept as an open space. The final negotiated price was £2,640,000, though not on a cash-down basis. Separate parcels or packages of the estate were to be purchased and paid for yearly over eight years interest-free — much to the advantage of Bournemouth — in what came to be called the 'Littledown package deal', starting in 1973. It was stated in the contract that Ellen or Edith, or both of them, were guaranteed the right to reside in the house and to farm the land until 31 March 1984, for the Corporation's advisers believed that neither of the two sisters was likely to live longer. After this date, Littledown House and land were due to be handed over to the Corporation.

However, there was an important proviso. If, by 31 March 1984, either Ellen or Edith or both of them still occupied Littledown House they were thenceforward to pay interest at seven per cent a year, on the entire £2,640,000. So, the Cooper Dean sisters, one or both, were given three years to a day to get out after the Corporation had produced the agreed price. Failure to do so committed them to pay interest in startling contrast to the terms of the sale, amounting to no less than £184,800 a year! It was, to put it midly, a no-nonsense agreement. We shall see, in due course, what the outcome was.

So, the agreement — 'the package deal' — was signed by both sisters. Neither of them relished disposing of the house and parkland which had been the family's home since 1798, but it was inevitable, an authentic case of *après nous, la déluge!* And so, in the light of subsequent building developments it would prove to be.

Not long after the sale, members of the Bournemouth County Borough Council proposed that the freedom of the borough should as a tribute be conferred on Ellen and Edith Cooper Dean and members of their family before them, for the way in which they had helped the town — and in many less conspicuous ways had helped the townspeople. The sisters were asked privately if they would accept the honour and they assented with pleasure.

Then came an unexpected turn of events. At a final meeting about it in the Council chamber, what the *Bournemouth Times* dubbed 'an uproar' took place. Labour members loudly opposed the proposal and walked out, declaring that the family had sold land to the Council at market value and that the award was unjustified — a view that wholly disregarded its philanthropy over the years.

Subsequently, however, the Council supported the proposal, but Ellen in particular had been deeply hurt by the manner and tone of the objections, so much so that when the offer was formally made she declined to accept it, and Edith followed suit. It was an unhappy episode in the Cooper Deans' long and open-handed relationship with Bournemouth. Could the town not do better now, as regards a family so intimately linked with its past history?

After the signing of the Littledown sale, Edith — and her faithful friend, 'Apple' — carried on farming there as before, content to remain to the last day on the land where she had lived most of her life. The happy problem that Ellen faced, living at the house near Henley, was whether to buy a farm for pleasure and as an investment, or racehorses, first. She and Sylvia were already looking at farms on the market in the Dorset area. The issue solved itself in 1973. Hearing that shipping magnate Jack Bilmeir's widow had died and that their country home, Parnham Park Farm, was on the market, they visited it. The 730 acres of rolling pasture and fine 16th century house captivated Ellen at once. Negotiations were successfully concluded and a year later, following extensive redecoration, she and Sylvia moved in. Ellen also bought 30 pedigree Hereford at pasture there, the nucleus of a herd that she decided to create in these lovely surroundings. Sylvia, whose parents and grandparents had been Dorset farmers, possessed a store of practical knowledge, so they would not be walking in the dark.

Meantime, another 60 acres, called 'the common', between

Edith (left) and Ellen Cooper Dean prepare to draw the first pints of ale, having formally opened in 1960 the public house named after them on the Holdenhurst Road started by the brewers Courage Limited.

the front of Littledown House and Harewood Avenue, had been excluded from the 'package deal' to prevent new housing development creeping towards the House. Sheep once grazed there and a noted butcher sold 'Littledown lamb', famed for quality and flavour.

It occurred to Ellen that these 60 acres should also be sold now. Her share of the proceeds would help to finance her horse racing and leave something over for the farm. But Edith did not approve. 'Why should we?' she said. 'In no time at all we would be faced with a rash of new houses below Littledown. That's the last thing we want.' Instead she offered to buy Ellen's share of the land at the market price, and this was done. Ellen received half the cash value of the land from Edith, to whom the title to Ellen's share was transferred. It was also agreed between the sisters at this time that 15 acres nearby, called 'the valley', should be given to the Corporation for the local community as a permanent open space for recreation and pleasure.

Farming remained as ever, Edith's main interest. In 1974 she bought another farm of 665 acres near Salisbury for which she engaged as manager, a friend, Robert Gates, who was already managing Littledown. At that time she received a proposal that she should make a substantial gift of money to a local girls' private secondary school to save it from having to close down. Uplands School, Parkstone, with its 19 acres of land, was threatened with closure in the very near future because the land-owner, the Church of England Education Corporation, wished to raise money for its work by selling this valuable land to developers for a housing scheme.

It was proposed to Edith that she should form an educational trust to buy the land and refurbish the school. The field of education was new to her, but she visited the school, liked it and set the wheels in motion. The outcome was the formation of the Edith Cooper-Dean Foundation, through which, at a cost of several hundred thousand pounds, she purchased the site for the school and ensured its future. To complete the undertaking she spent another £100,000 upon new buildings. It was also agreed, at the request of Edith, who had unhappy memories of her boarding school days, that it should be a day-school henceforward, with a limit of 250 girls.

Edith had never before involved herself with education, so what were her reasons for doing so? 'I am not as young as I was and I wanted to do some good with my money,' she said simply. 'Until I was asked to help I knew nothing at all about the school, but having looked over it I wanted to help it survive.' The school has never ceased to benefit from this act of generosity.

While farming and the school occupied Edith, farming and horse-racing began to absorb Ellen. It was in 1974 at the age of 75 that she embarked on her racing venture. And surely, she must have been the only race-horse owner of either sex in the long history of racing to have braved its hazards at an age when most people prefer to look back on their past lives and memories, rather than face the uncertainties of fresh

Ellen Cooper Dean (right) caresses her horse Maynooth after it had won the Salisbury Stakes at Salisbury racecourse on 26 June 1975. Trainer Ian Balding in straw hat looks on with satisfaction.

challenges. Behind her quiet personality Ellen was a mettlesome woman, and after a confined life she was determined to live as fully as her last years allowed.

With advice from the trainer Ian Balding — then the Queen's trainer — she had bought her first horses, including Annaray, in 1974, and won with her at Salisbury that season. It was an encouraging beginning, and Ellen looked forward to owning more horses in 1975. Meanwhile, she was informed that the Hampshire County Cricket Club were trying hard to raise money for a modern score board at the Dean Park Cricket Ground. Remembering the many happy times her father and grandfather had spent watching cricket there, she decided to make a gift of a new board to the club in his memory. She ascertained the price, which was not small, and sent the club secretary a cheque big enough to cover the cost of purchase and construction. A few months later, in appreciation of her generosity, the club unveiled a plaque on the scoreboard to commemorate the gift.

Her plans for next season's racing were well advanced.

Fast Frigate, ridden by jockey John Matthias, wearing Ellen's colours of yellow with a red star back and front and on helmet, wins the Milburn Maiden Stakes for her at Sandown on 21 July 1976.

Through Ian Balding, who travelled to Ireland for the purpose, she bought over the years several more two-year-olds — Maynooth, Yorker, Run-the-Gauntlet, Paul Diver, Parnham Prince, Ripalong, Fast Frigate, Lorison, Singing Sue and Musical Mermaid. It was a substantial stable, with a heavy bill but owning and racing these fine horses, among whom Fast Frigate was her favourite, seeing them sometimes sprint first past the post, gave her extraordinary pleasure, perhaps the greatest pleasure in her life, as she once remarked. Unhappily, this pleasure was not unmixed. Her arthritis was becoming so painful that even being driven by car to race meetings became something of an ordeal. When ordering a Rolls-Royce at this time she had to have a special seat fitted to make getting in and out less irksome.

Eventually, she agreed to have an artificial hip replacement. The operation was successful, but owing to her age — she was then 76 — she was unable to walk easily or to attend races as often as hitherto, although her interest never flagged — nor her generosity. Through Ian Balding she learned that the

Stable Lads' Welfare Trust wished to build retirement homes, but were having financial problems. Thereupon, she made a gift of money towards the cost of the project. Ian Balding then donated several acres of land, upon which eventually the homes were built. They have been a great boon ever since.

Edith, through the blazing summer of 1976 and the less agreeable one of 1977, went on determinedly farming. Ellen more and more felt the effects of her 78 years, but Edith, though just three years younger seemed as vigorous as ever and tried to live her life strenuously, as she had always done.

Then suddenly, one day at Littledown in June 1977, she had a severe heart attack and died. Her unexpected death was a great shock to her many friends, especially to 'Apple', who had been her close companion for some 30 years. Edith Cooper Dean was praised widely for her generosity and for the good she had done in the town. Her personal estate was valued at over £2 million. After the payment of heavy death duties, substantial legacies went to friends, and staff at her farms. She also left valuable furniture, silver, pictures and other articles at Littledown to 'Apple', who, some three months later, put them up for auction, and thereby gained a small fortune. Family portraits dating back to the late 18th century were included in the sale, but they were bid for successfully on Ellen's behalf and put back on the walls at Littledown. Edith left the residue of her estate to Robert Gates.

Was Ellen deeply affected by her sister's death? She was sorrowful, but she did not grieve deeply, for they had never been greatly fond of each other. The gulf of discordant feelings between them was deep and far-reaching. By nature, Edith was a dominating woman. For Ellen, in all ways the oppposite, it was at times a bruising relationship from which she had suffered.

But it was a shock to find herself suddenly the only living member of the ancient Cooper Dean family.

CHAPTER 14

Farewell, Littledown

THE HORIZONS OF Ellen's life widened after the death of Edith, and the departure of 'Apple' from Littledown to a house given to her in the will. For the first time she was able to live in and look after Littledown as she wished. Indeed, until 31 March 1984 she was its legal custodian. She was also entitled in due course to occupy and manage the two farms, Littledown and the Manor Farm, taking them over from Edith's executors.

But she possessed in Parnham Park Farm a home and an establishment of which she had grown extremely fond. Edith's unexpected death therefore faced her with a dilemma: did she really wish to leave Parnham, where she had already increased her pedigree Hereford herd, for Littledown? Beautiful and appealing as it was, it had by no means always been an unmixed source of pleasure.

The decision was made even harder because everything in the house — furniture, carpets, curtains, bed linen, china, glassware, kitchen utensils — had been auctioned by 'Apple', so that she would have to refurnish at least part of it. Simpler, therefore, was the prospect of committing herself fully to Parnham and leaving Littledown to the past, so that it became only a memory, but this she could not bear. Her old home remained precious, source of too many happy memories of childhood for her simply to leave it to decay or be vandalised; houses, she knew, need to be occupied to be kept alive. She decided that she would have to compromise. She would live in both houses, on alternate weeks as the mood took her, having re-furnished Littledown as she wanted. So, it was done. She and Sylvia thenceforward motored the 45 miles between

Bournemouth and west Dorset as they felt inclined. And Ellen enjoyed being for the first time mistress of her old home.

But she was not only concerned just with arrangements for her personal benefit. As an old lady of 78, though with a youthful mind, she felt acutely the wide gulf that separated her own life, with the power she possessed to satisfy her every reasonable desire, from that of the majority, especially that large section of people who were often deprived of a satisfying life. Compassion for them she had always felt and had on many occasions provided money where it was needed. Yet she did not believe that any radical changes in the social system would get rid of poverty and deprivation. It seemed to her that there was no evidence anywhere throughout the world to support this belief. Living standards appeared to her to rise where efficient private enterprise prevailed.

She decided that she herself must in some way use a substantial sum of her own resources to provide financial help where it was needed, perhaps by founding a trust devoted to the purpose. She thought about the project and for some months discussed it with Sylvia. Her decision finally to act came early in 1977, before Edith's death, when the payments for Littledown from Bournemouth Corporation had begun to accumulate — despite her spending on racing and the farm at Parnham.

She began talks with her professional advisers about how best to accomplish what she desired. The outcome was the decision to found a charity, with clearly defined purposes. It was drafted, agreed and, in March 1977, signed by herself as the founder, or grantor, with Sylvia and the advisers as trustees. The trust deed declared that it should be called the Alice Ellen Cooper Dean Foundation, established for the purpose of 'the relief of poverty, distress and sickness, the advancement of education and religion and other charitable purposes of benefit to the community'.

Ellen created an endowment fund by transferring to the

Ellen Cooper Dean's charm is fittingly captured in this fine portrait of her in oils by her friend, the artist Mara MacGregor. It is regarded as a fitting memorial to the last of a family whose members contributed so much to Bournemouth over the years.

(MORRIS BENJAMIN)

trust, titles to a number of her freehold properties in Bourne-mouth, together with the rents and profits arising from them. The trust deed declared that the trustees should have full discretion to use the income from the fund 'upon such chari-table trusts and for such charitable purposes within the objects of the Charity' as the trustees should determine, 'provided always that the endowment fund and the income thereof shall be used or paid exclusively for charitable purposes'. The trustees were also given entire control and management of the trust's freehold properties, income and administration.

Signing the trust and deed of gift documents, Ellen was happy in the knowledge that she had created an undertaking whose resources over the years to come would inevitably grow, thus long after her own death continuing to help future gener-ations. So pleased was she that in her will, written at this time, she bequeathed to it a further £200,000.

Ellen's charitable trust began early in its life helping various local charities; over the years they were joined by numerous national ones. These now include: the Queen Elizabeth Foun-dation for the Disabled, King George's Fund for Sailors, HRH Princess Christian Nursing Home, the Royal National Life-boat Institution, the British Red Cross, The Animal Health Trust, British Wildlife, the Boys' Brigade, the Gunnar Nilson Cancer Treatment Campaign, the Injured Jockey Trust, the Mental Health Foundation, the Sue Ryder Stable Lads' Trust, the Salvation Army, the YWCA, Salisbury Cathedral Spire, the Veterinary Benevolent Society and the York Minster Appeal. Since its formation, the Charity's capital value has increased fivefold.

Ellen not only gave money to people in need, but also kindness of a practical kind. Edith's executors, having tempor-arily taken over management of the farms, had been obliged to serve notice on the farm workers ending their employment and even their residence in estate cottages. In due course, Ellen be-came entitled to occupy and manage the farms, and with Syl-via's help began to do so. She was then informed by the ten-ants — some of whom she had known since childhood — that they had been given notice. Anxious about their welfare she at once set about re-engaging or compensating them.

But this kind-heartedness had an unpleasant sequel. On 21

October 1977 the weekly newspaper, the *Bournemouth Times,* carried a report on the front page which could be read as implying that she herself had dismissed the farm workers, thus behaving in a heartless and inconsiderate manner towards them and leaving them in a state of insecurity and uncertainty about their future.

Ellen felt that she had been libelled, and instituted proceedings against the newspaper. The action was heard in the High Court in April 1978. Ellen's counsel, Mr Richard Walker, told Mr Justice Park that his client did not seek damages and would be content with an apology and payment of her legal costs. On behalf of the newspaper, the Judge was told that it had never been intended to convey in the report the imputation to which Miss Cooper Dean objected, although it was now recognised that this was a possible interpretation. The owners of the newspaper nevertheless apologised in court and agreed to pay her legal costs. Ellen then considered that her name was cleared and the action settled to her satisfaction.

Meanwhile, with Sylvia's help she supervised the management of the three farms, liking nothing more than to drive round the pastures and yards in the mornings to view the animals and the work in progress. She entered a bull and a heifer in the Devon County Show competitions in May, 1978 and won a double success. Her two-year-old heifer, Yondover Silk, both won the first prize for heifers born in 1976 and was judged female champion and reserve-breed champion. Her two-year-old bull, Ddol Loyal, won the first prize in the large bull class. It was also male champion and breed champion, for which it won the Hubert Challenge Cup.

To complete this triumph, Ellen was awarded the novice tankard — because she had not previously won a first prize at the show. It was believed to be the first time that this trophy had been awarded to an owner with both champion and reserve champion of breed at the same time. She was proud of and delighted with the win, but not being a beer drinker she passed on the tankard to her herd manager.

By the end of 1979, at the age of 80, Ellen found ownership of this pedigree herd of cattle, as well as three farms, two homes, a stable of racehorses and attention to the management of her Cooper Dean Estates, rather too much for the energy

Shortly before leaving Littledown House for good, Ellen Cooper Dean with her Labrador, Daisy, sits in her drawing-room alone with her memories of the past. *(Evening Echo)*

she could muster. Something would have to go and she reviewed the possibilities. Most demanding, in terms of time and money were the horses, but owning and racing them during the past five years had given her almost a new life, so she was loth to part with them. Yet, she knew that in order to try to conserve her life she must retrench. So, in 1979, she embarked on what she knew would be her last season's racing, then announced that she would be retiring as an owner and that her horses were up for sale. Before the end of the year they were all gone. It made her sad to realise that henceforward she would be watching other owners' horses racing, and mainly on television, for her arthritis made travelling to racecourses an uncomfortable experience.

Nevertheless, for the next two years she continued the regular trips by road between Parnham and Littledown in her chauffeur-driven Rolls, insisting in doing so that she had no wish to appear pretentious. 'I know I have a Rolls,' she used to say, 'but I have it for sheer comfort. I have very bad arthritis and can travel comfortably in it.'

The appeal of Littledown for her grew as time passed. She feared that after her death anything could happen to it. But even though she no longer had to spend time and energy on her racehorses, her other interests and obligations, added to the driving back and forth imposed severe physical strain, and it told on her. In October 1982, she had a heart attack. She miraculously survived it and recovered but with much less physical strength she had henceforward to live quietly at Parnham, relinquishing Littledown, although it was not due to be taken over by the Corporation for another 15 months.

Ellen and Sylvia made a farewell visit, having already given instructions for everything of value — furniture, curtains, carpets, pictures — to be removed and taken to Laverstock, a house she owned in Dorset. The removal men were loading the last of them, checking with an inventory, when they arrived. Leaning heavily on her stick, Ellen walked painfully into the house with Sylvia, past the bare walls, through the empty passages and echoing rooms, knowing that she was the last of her family to be present, then and for ever, since William Dean built his fine house 185 years ago. Laboriously, she climbed the splendid staircase, and looked out of her bedroom window once more. Visions of her father and mother walking together over the lawns touched her, linked with the melancholy knowledge that she herself had unwittingly become the agent of final change. Would the house survive the change of ownership, she wondered, or have to make way for a new building of shining glass? And what of the park, where the deer used to graze? Soon, it would be engulfed in a wave of little villas. It was perhaps the saddest day in her life. 'Times have changed,' she said again and again to Sylvia. 'I have to realise it.'

A caretaker moved in next day to look after the house until it was due to be handed over. That date, as we know, was to be 31 March 1984, so, in good time, the Corporation was informed in accordance with the agreement that possession of the house would then be theirs. The keys were handed over on April 3rd to the mayor of Bournemouth, councillor Mrs Jeanne Curtis, by Sylvia, deputising at this historic little

The mayor of Bournemouth in 1984, councillor Mrs Jeanne Curtis (right) receives the Littledown House keys on 31 March from Miss Sylvia Bowditch, deputising for Ellen, who was then unwell.

(Photo: MORRIS BENJAMIN)

ceremony for Ellen, who was not strong enough to undertake it herself, or even to venture out at all.

She died in her sleep eleven days later on 14 April and was buried in Holdenhurst churchyard. A service of thanksgiving for this last member of an ancient family, the almost forgotten benefactors of Bournemouth, was held in St. John's Church, Holdenhurst, at noon on Saturday, 5 May 1984. Apart from various minor legacies, she left her property, including the Cooper Dean Estates, to Sylvia Bowditch, who for the past 21 years had enabled her to live happily.

★   ★   ★

The Cooper Dean family is remembered in Bournemouth today only by the older generation. In a few years it is likely that to all but a handful of local historians the name will convey nothing. One reason for this stems from the modest character of the family over the years. They evidently had no wish for recognition or public honours in return for their benevolence. Social embellishments did not interest them. Despite their wealth, they were content in the 19th and 20th centuries to be as they were in the 18th century, a rich but simple family of yeoman origin. This reserve has persuaded Bournemouth Corporation over the years to accept them at what seemed to be their own valuation. If the Cooper Deans were content to make generous gifts of land without public recognition, then so be it. Such seems to have been the negative attitude of the local authority in response to their help for the town and the townspeople.

The family's final act of goodwill came as we know, in 1973, when Ellen and Edith Cooper Dean sold Littledown House and 136 acres to the Corporation for £2,640,000, payable by eight annual interest-free instalments; then, in 1978, another 45 acres between Harewood Avenue and Littledown House for £765,000 , both far below market price. The subsequent profit for Bournemouth has been considerable. The Corporation was able to sell the 60 acres to a building consortium for no less than £3½ million, thus making a profit of £2,735,000, a much-needed contribution towards the cost of its lavish International Centre on the foreshore.

Then, in 1984, it exchanged with Chase Manhattan Bank Littledown House and 28 acres of accompanying land for the nearby Wessex Fields site, plus £1 million towards the cost of the recreational Littledown Park, an enterprise with a multi-purpose sports hall, swimming pool, squash courts, cricket pitches and other sports facilities that it has created. At a cost of £100,000, Chase has refurbished Littledown House and,

Overleaf:
An aerial photograph in 1985 shows Littledown House (centre right) in a belt of trees with (centre) Chase Manhattan Bank's new European headquarters building and (left) a housing estate in course of construction. (KITCHENHAM LIMITED)

Littledown House today, refurbished with great care by Chase Manhattan Bank, N.A. in 1986. Necessary work included a new roof, raised 12 inches to give a ceiling height of 7 feet in top rooms, and the strengthening with invisible steel struts of a fine cantilever staircase in the entrance hall. The bank has allocated part of the house to the Bournemouth General Hospital Appeal Fund as campaign headquarters.

spending another £30 million, developed the site as its European headquarters, giving permanent employment to several hundred local people and increasing Bournemouth's repute as a commercial finance market. The Wessex Fields site has brought the Corporation additional profit.

All this has stemmed from the unproclaimed goodwill and generosity of the Cooper Deans. Holdenhurst, whence they originated, is called 'the forgotten village'. Let them not become 'the forgotten family'.

Bibliography

Unpublished

Legal documents from the 17th, 18th and 19th centuries concerning the Dean family of Holdenhurst.

Bournemouth Corporation archives: records of land transactions with the Cooper Dean family.

Hampshire County Archives, Winchester: Holdenhurst Parish records: copy of the Christchurch and Holdenhurst Inclosure Award, 1805.

Published

Bright's Illustrated Guide to Bournemouth, 1886.

Bournemouth, 1810-1910, C.H. Mate & Charles Riddle, *W. Mate & Sons, 1910.*

The Book of Bournemouth, David and Rita Popham, *Barracuda Books, 1985.*

Contracts & Contacts, Ernest Fox, *Estates Gazette Ltd.*

Dorset Smugglers, Roger Gutridge, *Dorset Publishing Co, 1984.*

A History of Bournemouth, Elizabeth Edwards, *Phillimore, 1981.*

Diaries, James Harris, 1st Earl of Malmesbury.

A History of Dorset, John Hutchins, *1803.*

Literary Recollections, Richard Warner, *1830.*

Holdenhurst, Mother of Bournemouth, Kathleen M. Chiver, *Bournemouth Local Studies Publications, 1956.*

Memoirs of An ex-Minister, 3rd Earl of Malmesbury, *Longmans, 1884.*

My Life & Recollections, Hon. Grantley Berkeley, *Vol. 2, 1865.*

Social History of the Peoples of the Southern Counties, George Roberts, *1856.*

The Visitors' Guide to Bournemouth & Its Neighbourhood, 1840, 1842 and 1850.

Notes On Isaac Gulliver, V.J. Adams.

The Story of Bournemouth, David S. Young, *Robert Hale, Ltd., 1957.*

The Spas of England, Dr A.B. Granville, *1842.*

The Bournemouth Evening Echo.

The Hampshire Advertiser, 1838.

The Poole Herald, 1852.

Index

215